Sanjeev Kapoor's

Low Calorie
Vegetarian
Cookbook

Sanjeev Kapoor's

Low Calorie Vegetarian Cookbook

In association with Alyona Kapoor

Nutritional information in association with Dr. Mrs. Sujata Udeshi (Ph.D.)
Food Scientist, Nutritionist, Dietitian

POPULAR PRAKASHAN

POPULAR PRAKASHAN PVT. LTD.
35-C, Pt. Madan Mohan Malaviya Marg
Tardeo, Mumbai-400 034.

First Published 2001
First Reprint November 2001
Second Reprint February 2002
Third Reprint June 2003
Fourth Reprint May 2004

(3640)

ISBN - 81-7154-888-1

Printed in India
by Alert Packaging House Pvt. Ltd.
326, A to Z Industrial Estate
Ganpatrao Kadam Marg, Lower Parel
Mumbai 400 013 and
Published by
Ramdas Bhatkal
for Popular Prakashan Pvt. Ltd.
35-C, Pt. Madan Mohan Malaviya Marg
Tardeo, Mumbai-400 034.

AUTHOR'S NOTE

The overwhelming response of my first book gave me the encouragement and confidence to do something different. Added to this was my desire to make food popular for all types of persons whether fighting fit and leading normal healthy lives or those facing dietary restrictions due to health reasons. The result was my second book - *Khazana of Healthy Tasty Recipes* followed by *Khana Khazana: A Celebration of Indian Cookery*. All my books have been received well in the market. There seems to be a never-ending demand for recipes for all occasions.

Though my second book *Khazana of Healthy Tasty Recipes* was full of well balanced low calorie recipes there were many who could not quite relate to the title 'Healthy Tasty Recipes' and still asked for 'Low Calorie Recipes'. One reason for this was perhaps because the normal understanding is that to lose weight or to maintain a steady weight one has to depend on low calorie food. The other reason could be because healthy food is normally interpreted as something that is not tasty and has to be consumed due to compulsions put forth by the dietary restrictions. Let me first assure you that all food is healthy food and secondly there is no food which is tasteless. Every food item in itself has a taste of its own and contains certain nutrients that are beneficial to our health.

Healthy food would normally be defined as food that helps keep one in good health. It means the food should have adequate quality nutrients. All the food must meet the daily requirement of various nutrients like carbohydrates, vitamins and minerals that the body needs. But it is imperative to understand that to keep oneself in good health one has to keep an eye on the quantities that are consumed. The emphasis on quantity is because howsoever good a food may be, excess of anything can have adverse effect. However different body structures have different needs and hence each individual has to select his diet according to the demands of his body depending on age, physique and occupation.

Sedentary lifestyles and virtually no time to exercise forces many to go in for foods that are low in calories. This compilation is the result of the demand and need for a book on 'Vegetarian Low Calorie Recipes'. We have used some of the low calorie vegetarian recipes from my earlier book *Khazana of Healthy Tasty Recipes* while others have been created specially for this book. I have not only taken care to see that their calorie content is low but also given a lot of importance to the taste. However, while talking of 'low calorie food' it is essential to understand the meaning of the word calorie. Calories are simply units of energy measurement. The ideal situation is when you take in the essential amount of calories per day and burn off a like amount which happens when your body is functioning well. So if you consume more calories than what your body requires, the extra gets deposited and eventually results in weight gain. And excess weight can lead to numerous health problems. A thumb rule that always works for a person living in city conditions is to have about 30 calories per kilo of ideal body weight.

Nutrition apart a lot of attention should be given to how we prepare our food. Just as a child responds positively to love and affection and does what we ask him to do, food too rises to our expectations when treated likewise. If we prepare our food with love, affection and passion, there is no reason why the food should not satiate our taste buds.

All said and done, ultimately the key words to maintaining a healthy life are diet, attitude and exercise, which should work harmoniously.

At the end of each recipe nutritional facts have been given. Calorie is a unit of energy. Protein, Fat, Carbohydrate and Fibre are expressed in grams. Our nutritionist Dr. Sujata Udeshi has taken this opportunity to present some nutritional aspects of any one ingredient used in that recipe. In some pages there are notes on the method of cooking, or even simple things like seasoning and garnishing and on health.

All recipes serve four and the portion size of the serving takes into account the fact that the meal would be shared by a group of people. The calories mentioned with each recipe refer to the calories in a single serving.

An effort has been made to present information based on scientific reference and facts. However, this information is to be treated as generic and is not intended to advise or cure illness.

Slim with taste !

ACKNOWLEDGEMENTS

A. I. Kazi
Aditi Mehta
Anand Bhandiwad
Anil Bhandari
Ashok Bhat
Asmita Mohite
Capt. K. K. Lohana
Chef Ganesh
Chef Rajiv Julka
Chefs of India
Clea PR
Dr. Chetan Bhatt
Dr. Meena and Ram Prabhoo
Dr. Sujata Udeshi
Ergotech Studio, Pune
Ganesh Pednekar
Harpal Singh Sokhi
Jayakumar
Jaydeep Chaubal
Jijesh Gangadharan
Jyotsna and Mayur Dvivedi
Kiran Mhatre
Lohana Khaandaan
Mr. and Mrs. Kalyanpur
National School of Cooking
Neelima Acharya
Neena Murdeshwar
Pooja and Rajeev Kapoor
Priyakshi Rajguru Goswami
Rajeev Matta
Rajesh Choudhary
Rajiv Attri
Rama B. Udeshi
Rutika Samtani
Sakshi Udeshi
Sanjiv and Namrata Bahl
Shyam Kulkarni
Smeeta Bhatkal
Sunit Purandare
The Yellow Chilli, Ludhiana
Tripta Bhagattjee
Zee Television

CONTENTS

SALADS

Salads are a symphony of tastes and textures where individual flavours are recognized but the combined effect is pleasant harmony. Though not new to the world of food, their use has broadened recently. For salads can not only be served as appetizers but also as a main course. They play the dual role of complementing a meal as well as being a dieter's salvation. Salads mean lots of eating without loads of calories. Chewing salad satisfies the feeling of hunger. With oil-less dressings, they are often very low in calories yet packed with nutritive contents and roughage. Besides, a bowl of colourful vegetables add to the aesthetics of a beautifully laid table.

The vegetable-based salads are rich in vitamins like B complex, C, Beta-carotene and folic acid. Minerals like calcium, iron and potassium are also present in good amounts especially in greens like lettuce, celery and broccoli. When eaten raw or just tossed in some seasoning they provide a lot of roughage or fibre and therefore play an important role in preventing constipation, lowering cholesterol and triglyceride, decreasing absorption of sugar and even in protecting from certain cancers. Beans and sprout-based salads are high in proteins, riboflavin and vitamin C.

For many health conscious people soup and salad or soup, salad and a low calorie dessert make up a satisfying and filling meal.

HEALTHY SALAD IN GARLIC DRESSING

INGREDIENTS

Spinach	16-20 leaves	Malt vinegar	2 tblspns
Lettuce	16-20 leaves	Virgin olive oil	1 tblspr
Red pepper	1 medium sized	Mustard paste	1 tblspr
Tomatoes	4 medium sized	Salt	to taste
Pineapple	4 slices	Black pepper powder	¼ tspr
Baby corns	6-8	Brown sugar	1 tspr
Garlic	8-10 cloves		

METHOD OF PREPARATION

NUTRITIONAL INFORMATION

Calories	65
Proteins	4.8
Fat	1.5
Carbohydrates	8
Fibre	1

*Though corn is considered a grain cereal, **baby corn** comes under vegetables. It can be eaten raw and finds a place in many salads. It is a good source of complex carbohydrates and also supplies some minerals and vitamins.*

1. Wash the spinach and lettuce leaves in running water thoroughly. Drain and tear them roughly.
2. Wash and wipe red pepper dry. Apply very little oil on the red pepper and roast in a very hot oven till blisters form on the pepper. Alternatively you can roast red pepper on an open flame also. Cool a little and peel the top skin. Halve the pepper, deseed and cut into one and a half inch long strips.
3. Wash and cut tomatoes into halves and deseed. Cut them into one and a half inch long strip. Cut pineapple slices into one and a half long strips.
4. If the baby corns are tender, cut them lengthwise into strips and use raw. Otherwise blanch them in salted water for five to seven minutes, cool and use.
5. Peel and chop garlic. Combine malt vinegar, virgin olive oil, garlic, mustard paste, salt, brown sugar and black pepper powder.
6. Mix red pepper, baby corn, tomatoes and pineapple. Gently mix with lettuce and spinach leaves. Add the prepared dressing on to the salad and toss it. Serve cold.

LEAFY GREENS WITH APPLE AND CARAWAY VINAIGRETTE

INGREDIENTS

Cabbage .... ¼ small sized
Iceberg lettuce .... 1 medium sized
Leaf lettuce ....
(preferably Romaine) .... 1 bunch
Tender spinach leaves .... 16-20 leaves
Tender radish leaves 8-10
Dill leaves .... ½ cup

Dressing
Caraway seeds .... 1 tspn

Apple juice .... ½ cup
Olive oil .... 1 tblspn
Red wine vinegar .... 4 tblspns
Paprika or red chilli powder . ¼ tspn
Honey .... 1 tspn
Black pepper (crushed) .... ½ tspn
Salt .... to taste

METHOD OF PREPARATION

1. Roast the caraway seeds on a dry *tawa*, cool and crush well.
2. Mix all the dressing ingredients in a bottle, close tightly and shake well. Refrigerate till you require.
3. Wash cabbage and cut into one inch sized pieces.
4. Clean and thoroughly wash iceberg lettuce, leaf lettuce, tender spinach, tender radish, dill leaves in running water, then trim and refresh in chilled water.
5. Tear the leaves into bite size pieces, mix well and refrigerate to keep them crisp.
6. Just before serving, pour the prepared dressing and toss. Serve cold.

NUTRITIONAL INFORMATION

Calories	80
Proteins	1.4
Fat	4.2
Carbohydrates	12
Fibre	0.8

Dill *is a leafy vegetable commonly known as* Soowa *or* Shepu. *It is rich in Beta-carotene, iron, calcium, and Vitamin B complex. It is advisable to first wash all leafy vegetables under running water and then cut, to prevent loss of water-soluble nutrients.*

Dill leaves are known to aid digestion. They also promote the flow of breast milk in lactating mothers.

T I P   *If Red wine vinegar is not easily available, use malt vinegar instead.*

PEPPERY CORNS AND TOMATO SALAD

INGREDIENTS

Whole corn kernels .... 2 cups
Yellow capsicum (optional) ....
.... 1 medium sized
Green capsicum .... 2 medium sized
Pineapple .... 4 slices
Tomatoes .... 3 medium sized

Green chillies 1-2
Mint leaves .... ½ cup
Pepper corns 15-20
Lemon juice .... 2 tblspns
Salt .... to taste

METHOD OF PREPARATION

1. Boil corn kernels in salted water until soft. Drain thoroughly and cool. You may also use precooked canned corn kernels or sweet corn niblets. Wash them thoroughly before use.
2. Wash, halve, deseed yellow capsicum and green capsicum and then dice into one cm. sized pieces. Similarly cut pineapple slices into one cm. sized pieces.
3. Wash tomatoes, cut into quarters, deseed and then dice into one cm. sized pieces.
4. Wash green chillies, remove stem and then chop them. Clean, wash and chop mint leaves. Crush pepper corns.
5. Combine corn kernels, yellow pepper, green pepper, tomatoes and pineapple. Stir in lemon juice and add crushed pepper corns, salt, chopped green chillies and chopped mint leaves.
6. Arrange in a serving dish and chill before serving.

MINTED MUSHROOMS

INGREDIENTS

Mushrooms .... 400 gms	Mint leaves .... 1 cup
Lemon juice .... 2 tblspns	Skimmed milk yogurt ...... 3 tblspns
Tomato .... 1 medium sized	Salt .... to taste
Cucumber .... 1 medium sized	Cabbage or lettuce leaves ..... 4 to 5

METHOD OF PREPARATION

1. Clean and wash mushrooms and then cut into quarters.
2. Put mushrooms in a thick-bottomed vessel along with lemon juice and a little salt. Stew them over low heat for ten minutes. Keep aside.
3. Wash, halve, deseed tomato and dice into one cm. sized pieces. Peel cucumber and dice it into one cm. sized pieces.
4. Clean, wash mint leaves, reserve one or two sprigs for garnishing and chop the rest.
5. Combine mushrooms with diced tomato, diced cucumber and chopped mint. Mix in skimmed milk yogurt and salt and toss lightly.
6. Serve on a bed of cabbage leaves or lettuce leaves garnished with a sprig of mint leaves.

NUTRITIONAL INFORMATION

Calories	60
Proteins	4.0
Fat	1.0
Carbohydrates	8
Fibre	0.7

Mint is a good source of Beta-carotene, iron, calcium, Beta-complex and Vitamin C. Usually mint is eaten uncooked in the form of dressing or chutney. There is a good amount of Vitamin C and B complex in green leafy vegetables, but they are destroyed on cooking. Hence it is a good practice to eat mint, green coriander and others in the uncooked form. Mint is also known to aid digestion.

FOUR BEAN SALAD

INGREDIENTS

White cow beans (*Chowli*) .... ¼ cup
Red kidney beans (*Rajma*) .... ¼ cup
Green grams (*Sabut Moong*) .... ¼ cup
French beans .... 100 gms
Onion .... 1 medium sized
Fresh coriander .... ½ cup

Mint .... ¼ cup
Green chillies 2
Ginger .... 1 one inch knob
Lemon juice .... 3 tblspns
Chaat Masala .... 1 ½ tspns

METHOD OF PREPARATION

1. Pick and wash white cow beans and kidney beans separately.
2. Soak them separately, overnight in plenty of water. Wash and soak *moong* for about two hours.
3. Boil the three beans separately in salted water till soft. Drain and let them cool.
4. String the French beans and cut into one-fourth inch pieces. Boil in salted boiling water till done. Drain immediately (you may reserve the cooking liquid to use as stock for some other recipe) and refresh with cold water. Drain and keep aside.
5. Peel and cut onion into one-fourth inch sized pieces. Clean, wash, drain and chop green coriander and mint. Wash and chop green chillies finely. Peel and wash and chop it.
6. Dilute lemon juice with equal amount of water. Stir in chopped green coriander, mint leaves, green chillies, ginger and *chaat masala*. Shake well and refrigerate the dressing for at least an hour.
7. Mix all the cooked beans with diced onion and add the dressing. Toss the salad to evenly mix the dressing.

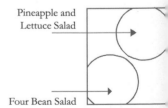

Pineapple and Lettuce Salad

Four Bean Salad

T I P *Do not hesitate to throw away the water in which you soak pulses as it is going to be more harmful than beneficial.*

SPICY PINEAPPLE BOAT

INGREDIENTS

Pineapple	1 medium sized	Pomegranate	½ medium sized
Apples	2 medium sized	Oranges	2 medium sized
Papaya	1 small sized	Lemon juice	1 tblspn
Green chillies	2-3	Ground black salt	to taste
Pears	2 medium sized	Orange juice	3 tblspns

METHOD OF PREPARATION

1. Halve the pineapple lengthwise. Scoop the flesh out without damaging the shell and cut the flesh into one cm. sized pieces.
2. Wash, core and cut apples into one cm. cubes.
3. Peel, halve, deseed and cut papaya into one cm. cubes.
4. Wash green chillies and grind to a coarse paste.
5. Wash and cut pears into one cm. cubes. Separate pomegranate pearls from the pomegranate.
6. Peel orange, remove segments, discard seeds and cut each orange segment into three pieces.
7. Mix all fruits with lemon juice, green chilli paste, ground black salt and orange juice. Serve this in the halved pineapple boats.

NUTRITIONAL INFORMATION

Calories	135
Proteins	1.5
Fat	0.7
Carbohydrates	31.8
Fibre	2.5

*Ripe **papaya** has a good amount of Vitamin C and Beta-carotene. The carotene gets converted to vitamin A in our bodies. Both vitamin C and Beta- carotene have anti-oxidant property. However, seeds of papaya should not be eaten along with the fruit as they contain a toxic substance called carpine in them. Papain enzyme present in papaya helps digestion.*

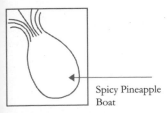

Spicy Pineapple Boat

T
I
P

Since this dish is rich in minerals like potassium, it can prevent muscle cramps.

PINEAPPLE AND LETTUCE SALAD

INGREDIENTS

Pineapple	6 slices	Honey	1 tblspn
Iceberg lettuce	16-20 leaves	Salt	to taste
Cucumber	2 medium sized	Dried mixed herbs	¼ tspn
Lemon juice	2 tblspns	Crushed pepper corns	1 tspn
Pineapple juice	3 tblspns	White pepper powder	¼ tspn

METHOD OF PREPARATION

1. Cut pineapple into three-fourth inch sized pieces.
2. Wash and keep iceberg lettuce in ice cold water for about fifteen minutes.
3. Peel cucumber, wash and cut into half lengthwise and remove seeds. Then cut cucumber into three-fourth inch sized pieces.
4. Mix lemon juice, pineapple juice, honey, salt, mixed herbs, crushed pepper corns and white pepper powder. Leave aside for at least fifteen minutes.
5. Tear lettuce leaves into bite-sized pieces and combine with pineapple and cucumber pieces.
6. Pour the dressing on the salad and toss lightly. Serve immediately.

TIP *Fresh herbs can either be sun-dried or can be dried in a warm oven. Store in an air-tight container or bottle for future use.*

ORIENTAL SALAD WITH FRESH ORANGE DRESSING

INGREDIENTS

Chinese cabbage ..... ½ medium sized
Snow peas/flat beans 8-10
Bean sprouts .... 2 cups
Red radish .... 2 medium sized
Carrots .... 2 medium sized
Capsicum .... 2 medium sized
Steamed rice .... ½ cup

For Dressing

Sesame seeds .... ½ tspn
Fresh orange juice .... ½ cup
Honey .... 1 tblspn
Refined oil .... 1 tblspn
Salt .... to taste
Pepper powder .... to taste
Red chillies whole (crushed) ..... ½ tspn

METHOD OF PREPARATION

1. Clean, wash and shred Chinese cabbage. Wash and trim the snow peas (or flat beans) and cut each into three pieces.
2. Peel and cut radish into half lengthwise and then thinly slice. Peel and cut carrots into half lengthwise and then thinly slice.
3. Wash, halve, deseed and cut capsicum into half inch sized triangles. Dry roast sesame seeds, cool and crush them a little.
4. For dressing take all the ingredients in an airtight container and shake so that they mix well.
5. Toss the prepared vegetables and steamed rice in a salad bowl with the dressing and serve crisp.

NUTRITIONAL INFORMATION

Calories	165
Proteins	6.6
Fat	6.9
Carbohydrates	26.3
Fibre	2

Orange is one of the most popular citrus fruits. Orange is a rich source of protective food nutrients like Vitamins A, B and C. Orange also contains a good amount of electrolytes like sodium, potassium and chloride. Regular consumption gives enough protection against cold and cough.

It increases body immunity. Eating whole orange rather than drinking orange juice is recommended since it has the added benefit of fibre.

SLIMMERS SALAD IN NO OIL DRESSING

INGREDIENTS

Iceberg lettuce .... 1 bunch
Apples .... 2 medium sized
Watermelon (optional) ¼ small sized
Carrot .... 1 medium sized
Cucumber.............. 1 medium sized
Tomatoes .... 2 medium sized
Celery .... 1 stem
Orange 2
Capsicum .... 1 medium sized

Spring onions 2
Mint leaves .... a few sprigs
Garlic .... 6-8 cloves
Mustard seeds .... 1 tspn
Sea Salt .... 1 tspn
Pepper corns 8-10
Lemon juice .... 2 tspns
Malt vinegar .... 2 tspns

It is commonly believed that a salad dressing has a lot of oil or egg yolks and therefore adds extra calories to the dish. Basic French or English dressing has a higher proportion of oil and a lesser amount of vinegar or lemon juice. This is true for almost all the commercial dressings available in the market.

Try a no oil dressing with lemon juice, vinegar or even low fat or skimmed yogurt.

METHOD OF PREPARATION

1. Wash the lettuce, tear into bite size pieces and dip in ice cold water to make it crisp.
2. Wash, core the apples and cut into one inch cubes.
3. Cut, slice, peel and deseed the watermelon. Peel and wash the carrot. Peel, wash and deseed the cucumber; wash and deseed the tomatoes. Cut all into one inch sized cubes.
4. Wash and cut celery sticks into one inch sized pieces.
5. Skin orange, separate the segments and deseed them. Cut them into half.
6. Wash, deseed and cut capsicum into one inch cubes.
7. Wash the spring onions and cut the greens into one inch long pieces. Cut the onions into quarters and separate the layers.
8. Wash mint leaves, reserve some for garnishing and chop the remaining.
9. In a bowl, mix all the fruits and vegetables except iceberg lettuce and chopped mint leaves. Chill in the refrigerator for about ten minutes
10. For making the dressing, peel garlic cloves and crush them in a small mortar and pestle along with mustard seeds, sea salt, pepper corns, chopped mint leaves and lemon juice
11. Toss the salad with malt vinegar and the dressing. Serve the salad on a bed of crisp lettuce, garnished with mint sprigs.

CROSTINI

INGREDIENTS

Whole wheat loaf............................ ½
Olive oil .... 2 tblspns
Dry rosemary .... ½ tspn
Tomatoes................ 3 medium sized
Cucumber.............. 2 medium sized
Iceberg lettuce .... 1 bunch

Red bell pepper .... ½
Yellow bell pepper .... ½
Capsicum 1
Crushed pepper corns .... 1 tspn
Salt .... to taste

METHOD OF PREPARATION

1. Break loaf into small chunky pieces. Arrange them on a baking tray, sprinkle one tablespoon olive oil and dry rosemary and toast in a preheated oven at 160 degrees Celsius for thirty to forty-five minutes till crisp. Allow it to cool.
2. Wash, deseed and cut the tomatoes into one inch sized cubes. Wash, peel, deseed the cucumbers and cut into cubes. Wash the lettuce thoroughly under running water and tear into bite sized pieces.
3. Using a fork, grill the red and yellow bell peppers over direct flame till the outer skin gets charred. Remove from flame and transfer into cold water. Peel the skin and cut into one inch sized triangles.
4. Wash the capsicum, cut into two, remove seeds and cut into one inch sized triangles.
5. Mix all the vegetables in a large mixing bowl, add the toasted bread, olive oil, freshly crushed pepper corns and salt. Serve immediately.

NUTRITIONAL INFORMATION

Calories	115
Proteins	3.4
Fat	3.5
Carbohydrates	17.2
Fibre	0.9

*Apart from green capsicum, **bell pepper** (sweet pepper) is grown in shades of red, yellow, orange and purple. All sweet peppers are green before they are ripe. Peppers have a high moisture content (90-95%) and are low in calories (25 cals/100 gms)*

T I P *Stale bread, that is one or two days old, would give best results.*

VEGETABLE CRUDITES WITH GREEK YOGURT DIP

INGREDIENTS

Mint leaves .... ¼ cup
Garlic .... 4 cloves
Cherry tomatoes 8-10
Carrots .... 2 medium sized
White radish .... 1 medium sized
Red radish 4

Iceberg lettuce .... 8-10 leaves
Cucumbers .... 2 medium sized
Skimmed milk yogurt .... 4 cups
Sesame seeds (white) .... ¼ tspn
Lemon juice .... 1 tspn
Salt .... to taste

NUTRITIONAL INFORMATION

Calories	65
Proteins	3.2
Fat	0.8
Carbohydrates	12.5
Fibre	1.2

*Today, a variety of **dips** like sauces, ketchup, and chutneys are readily available in the market. Most of them have a high concentration of preservatives and added colour. Both preservatives and colour are known to have their ill-effects on health. So, as far as possible do go in for home-made dips and chutneys, which will be both safe and nutritious.*

METHOD OF PREPARATION

1. Clean mint leaves, wash and reserve some for decoration and chop the remaining. Peel and chop garlic finely.
2. Wash the cherry tomatoes and cut them into halves.
3. Peel carrots, wash and cut into finger sized pieces. Peel white radish, wash and cut into finger sized pieces.
4. Wash red radish and quarter each. Wash lettuce leaves and soak in chilled water. Peel cucumber, wash and cut into finger sized pieces.
5. Hang skimmed milk yogurt in a muslin cloth to remove excess water. Toast the sesame seeds lightly and cool.
6. Combine thick yogurt with chopped mint, lemon juice, white sesame seeds and garlic. Mix thoroughly. Add salt to taste and chill.
7. Just before serving drain the lettuce leaves and spread on a serving plate, arrange the prepared vegetables decoratively and serve with the chilled dressing.

CRUNCHY VEGETABLE SALAD

INGREDIENTS

Red cabbage	½ small	Roasted peanuts	½ cup
Green cabbage	½ small	Oil	2 tspns
Carrots	2 medium sized	Orange juice	5 tblspns
White radish	2 medium sized	Mustard paste	1 tspn
Capsicum	2 medium sized	Lemon juice	1 tblspn
Sprouted green gram (*Moong*)	2 cups	Salt	to taste
		White pepper powder	to taste

METHOD OF PREPARATION

1. Shred the red cabbage and green cabbage.
2. Peel, wash and grate carrots and white radish.
3. Wash, halve and deseed capsicums and then chop.
4. Wash bean sprouts and drain completely.
5. Crush roasted peanuts coarsely.
6. Mix oil, orange juice, mustard paste, lemon juice, salt and white pepper powder thoroughly. Keep aside in the refrigerator.
7. In a serving bowl arrange red cabbage at the bottom. Then layer with green cabbage, carrots, radish, capsicum and lastly bean sprouts. Chill in a refrigerator.
8. Spread roasted crushed peanuts on top.
9. Shake the dressing thoroughly and lace the salad with the dressing uniformly just before serving.

NUTRITIONAL INFORMATION

Calories	145
Proteins	6.7
Fat	6
Carbohydrates	17
Fibre	2

Carrot is an important source of Beta-carotene, choline and fibre (especially in raw form). It is also known to purify the blood and tone up the kidney. Beta-carotene that is converted to Vitamin A in the body, plays an important role in maintaining good vision, bone development, skin integrity, immunity, reproduction, and anti-cancer functions.

SOUPS

Soup is a liquid food made by cooking the main ingredients in water or stock to which herbs and spices are added for flavour and a thickening agent like cereal or cream is added to give the soup some body. Soups, like salads, can be a complementary dish or a full meal in itself. They can be made thin, clear and light that can be used as a starter or they can be thick, creamy and filling which, taken with a bread roll, can satiate the most demanding of appetites. Then again soups can be made hot and spicy that would ideally suit a cold and rainy day or can be had chilled on a hot summer afternoon.

An ideal soup should have a mild and not overpowering flavour and a pleasing and natural colour; it should be non-greasy and the seasoning should not be in excess but just enough (which can always be further enhanced to suit individual tastes). Creamy soups should have the consistency of fresh cream and clear soups should be slightly thicker than water.

Soups are highly nutritive, the actual values depending upon the ingredients used. Thin soups are lower in nutritive content when compared to the thick soups. A bowl of green pea soup is rich in protein whereas a bowl of spinach soup is rich in iron and can provide one third of an adult's daily requirement of the mineral.

Since very little or no fat need be used while preparing soup, it is certainly ideal for weight watchers or for those who have to follow a dietary restriction for medical reasons.

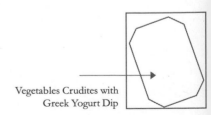
Vegetables Crudites with
Greek Yogurt Dip

BROCCOLI AND TOASTED ALMOND SOUP

INGREDIENTS

Broccoli .... 400 gms
Onion...................... 1 medium sized
Garlic .... 4 cloves
Celery stalk......................... 2 inches
Almonds 10-12

Vegetable stock or water...... 4 cups
Low fat milk............................ 1 cup
Salt .... to taste
White pepper powder .... to taste

METHOD OF PREPARATION

1. Cut broccoli into small florets and wash well. Soak in salted water for ten to fifteen minutes and drain.
2. Peel and roughly chop onion and garlic. Wash and chop celery stalk.
3. Broil or dry roast almonds on medium heat till almond skin changes its colour slightly. Remove from heat, cool and slice them into slivers.
4. Heat vegetable stock or water with chopped onion, garlic and celery. Bring it to a boil.
5. Add broccoli florets and continue to cook without covering the pan. Cook for five to seven minutes or till broccoli is tender.
6. Remove from fire, cool and puree it in a blender.
7. Add milk to pureed broccoli. Mix well. Bring to a boil again.
8. Add salt and white pepper powder to taste. Stir in toasted almond slivers and serve hot.

NUTRITIONAL INFORMATION

Calories	130
Proteins	7.2
Fat	4.3
Carbohydrates	9.5
Fibre	0.3

Broccoli looks like cauliflower but is dark green in colour. Broccoli being greener rates higher in nutritive value than cauliflower and is a good source of iron, phosphorous, vitamin A, ascorbic acid and riboflavin. The outer leaves of broccoli and cauliflower are much higher in nutritive value than the inner portions and should be used for cooking and salads. Broccoli has fibre and flavonoids which help in fighting cancer.

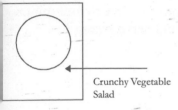

Crunchy Vegetable Salad

MIXED VEGETABLE SOUP

INGREDIENTS

Onion .... 1 medium sized
Carrot .... 1 medium sized
Potato .... 1 medium sized
Green cabbage .... ¼ medium sized
French beans 6-8
Fresh mushrooms 6-8
Capsicum .... 1 medium sized
Cauliflower florets .. 4-5 small sized

Oil .... 1 tblspn
Bay leaves 2
Whole meal flour .... 2 tspns
Salt .... to taste
White pepper powder .... to taste
Vegetable stock or water ...... 2 cups
Skimmed milk .... 2 cups

METHOD OF PREPARATION

1. Peel onion, carrot and potato. Chop them as fine as possible. Keep the chopped potatoes soaked in water to avoid discolouration. Clean, trim and finely chop the cabbage.
2. String french beans and chop them real fine. Wash mushrooms, drain well and chop them fine. Wash, halve, deseed and finely chop the capsicum.
3. Wash and grate cauliflower florets along with the tender part of the stem.
4. Heat oil in a thick-bottomed saucepan, add the bay leaves and chopped onion and sauté for two minutes over medium heat. Drain the chopped potatoes and add.
5. Add the chopped carrots, chopped mushroom, chopped cabbage, chopped french beans and grated cauliflower. Stir and cook on high heat for three to four minutes.
6. Sprinkle the whole meal flour and cook for two minutes, stirring continuously over medium heat or till flour starts giving a cooked aroma. Add salt and white pepper powder.
7. Stir in the vegetable stock and bring to boil. Add the chopped capsicum. Reduce heat and simmer till the vegetables are cooked and the soup reaches a fairly thick consistency.
8. Gradually stir in the skimmed milk and simmer for three to four minutes.
9. Remove the bay leaf, adjust the seasoning and serve piping hot.

VEGETABLE CLEAR SOUP

INGREDIENTS

Carrot	1 medium sized	Oil	½ tspn
Cabbage	¼ small	Bean sprouts	½ cup
Tomato	1 medium sized	Vegetable stock or water	5 cups
Capsicum	1 medium sized	Salt	to taste
Spinach	16-20 leaves	Lemon juice	1 tspn
Garlic	3-4 cloves	Crushed pepper corns	½ tspn
Mushrooms	80 gms		

METHOD OF PREPARATION

1. Wash and peel carrot, cut into two lengthwise. Make thin slices.
2. Wash and dice cabbage into one cm. sized pieces. Wash tomato, cut into quarters, remove seeds and dice it into one cm. sized pieces. Wash, halve and deseed capsicum. Dice into one cm. sized pieces.
3. Clean spinach leaves, wash thoroughly and chop roughly. Peel and slice garlic. Wash and slice mushrooms.
4. Heat oil in a pan and add sliced garlic. Stir-fry briefly.
5. Add mushrooms and all the vegetables except tomato. Add the bean sprouts. Stir in vegetable stock or water and salt to taste. Bring it to a boil and simmer for two minutes.
6. Add tomato pieces and stir in lemon juice and crushed pepper corns. Serve hot.

NUTRITIONAL INFORMATION

Calories	60
Proteins	3.3
Fat	0.5
Carbohydrates	9.5
Fibre	1.6

Cabbage, a low calorie leafy vegetable, belongs to the cruciferous family like cauliflower, radish, turnip, brussel sprouts, etc. There are wide varieties of cabbage. The regular or western variety is low in Beta-carotene and Vitamin C but the Chinese variety commonly called Chinese leaf is very high in both. Cabbage has fair amount of potassium and choline. Like other members of the cruciferous family, Chinese cabbage contains indols that are believed to fight cancer-producing cells.

TOMATO AND CARROT SOUP

INGREDIENTS

Onion .... 1 medium sized
Garlic .... 4 cloves
Carrots .... 2 medium sized
Tomatoes .... 8 medium sized
Potato .... 1 medium sized
Brown bread .... 2 slices

Vegetable stock or water ...... 2 cups
Bay leaf 1
Pepper corns 4-6
Fresh mint leaves 4-6
Salt .... to taste

METHOD OF PREPARATION

1. Peel and slice onion. Peel garlic and crush lightly. Scrub and wash carrots and chop them roughly. Wash tomatoes and chop them roughly. Peel and roughly slice the potato.
2. Toast brown bread slices in a toaster and cut toasted slices with a sharp knife into small square pieces. Alternately you can first cut the bread slices into small pieces and then dry roast in a non-stick pan, tossing continuously, till they are crisp.
3. Pressure cook all the prepared vegetables including onion and garlic along with one cup vegetable stock or water, bay leaf, pepper corns, mint leaves and salt.
4. Cool the cooked mixture. Ensure that the potato is thoroughly cooked.
5. Remove bay leaf and then puree it to a fine consistency in a blender.
6. Heat the pureed vegetables in a pan, add the remaining vegetable stock or water and adjust seasoning. Simmer for five minutes and serve with toasted brown bread croutons.

NUTRITIONAL INFORMATION

Calories	95
Proteins	2.8
Fat	1.5
Carbohydrates	18.8
Fibre	1.6

*It is customary to serve fried **croutons** with soup. But have you thought about the fact that sometimes these croutons can supply more calories than the soup itself! Using toasted croutons made from whole wheat bread will not only be a healthy alternative to fried croutons, but also to bread-sticks (made from refined flour or maida) which are frequently served with soup.*

SPINACH AND TOFU SOUP

INGREDIENTS

Tofu	100 gms	Vegetable stock	3 cups
Spinach	1 bunch	Light soya sauce	1 tblspn
Ginger	½ inch knob	Salt	to taste
Garlic	2 cloves	Pepper powder	to taste
Oil	1 tspn		

METHOD OF PREPARATION

1. Cut the tofu into one fourth inch thick slices and cut them into one inch sized triangles.
2. Wash the spinach leaves thoroughly under running water. Remove stems, roughly shred and keep them aside.
3. Peel and chop ginger and garlic. In a wok or frying pan, heat oil on high heat and sauté chopped ginger and garlic.
4. Add the vegetable stock and bring to a boil.
5. Add the tofu pieces and light soya sauce and when it comes to a boil reduce heat and simmer for about two minutes.
6. Add the shredded spinach leaves and simmer for a minute stirring gently. Remove the scum to make clear soup.
7. Add salt and pepper powder and serve hot.

NUTRITIONAL INFORMATION

Calories	40
Proteins	3.6
Fat	2.2
Carbohydrates	1.3
Fibre	0.3

Clear soups usually are light soups and can be served as a starter. They are excellent for recuperating patients who are advised a liquid diet.

Unlike other clear soups, which are usually both low in calories and in other nutrients, 'Spinach and tofu soup' is low in calories but high in other nutrients. Tofu is an excellent source of protein while spinach provides Betacarotene, B-complex, iron and calcium.

LETTUCE AND COTTAGE CHEESE BROTH

INGREDIENTS

Lettuce, preferably Romaine .. 20 leaves
Cottage cheese (*Paneer*) .... 150 gms
Carrot .... 1 medium sized
Spring onions 2
Ginger.................. 1 one inch knob
Refined oil....................... 1 ½ tspns
Vegetable stock .... 4 cups

Soya sauce .... 1 tblspn
Dry sherry .... 2 tblspns
Sugar .... 1 tspn
Salt .... to taste
Pepper powder .... to taste
Red chilli flakes .... 1 tspn
Vinegar .... 1 tspn

NUTRITIONAL INFORMATION

Calories	120
Proteins	7.7
Fat	8
Carbohydrates	6.2
Fibre	0.4

Vinegar is acetic acid and is a product of fermentation. Vinegar was originally used as a preservative. Over the years, however, it has also become a valued aromatic condiment. Today health-wise vinegar is a better choice as a preservative than most of the sodium salts that are commonly in use.

METHOD OF PREPARATION

1. Wash the lettuce under running water and tear roughly into small pieces.
2. Cut *paneer* into half inch sized cubes.
3. Wash, peel and slice carrots thinly. Wash and cut spring onions into diagonal slices. Chop the spring onion greens. Peel and cut ginger into juliennes.
4. Heat a non-stick pan and sauté *paneer* on high heat adding very little oil and tossing continuously until golden brown. Remove and transfer to a kitchen towel.
5. Heat remaining oil in the same pan and sauté spring onions, carrot slices and ginger juliennes for half a minute.
6. Add vegetable stock and cook on high heat. Add soya sauce and dry sherry, season with sugar, salt and pepper. Add *paneer* and lettuce. Mix well.
7. Stir in red chilli flakes and vinegar. Serve piping hot garnished with chopped spring onion greens.

SOUTHERN ITALIAN VEGETABLE SOUP

INGREDIENTS

Carrot	1 medium sized	Fresh basil	6-8 leaves
Potatoes	2 medium sized	Olive oil	1 tspn
Cabbage	¼ small sized	Salt	to taste
Tomatoes	2 medium sized	White pepper powder	to taste
Onion	1 medium sized	Macaroni	¼ cup
Garlic	4 cloves	Vegetable stock or water	4 cups
Celery	1 inch stalk		

METHOD OF PREPARATION

1. Wash and peel the carrot and chop it into very small dices.
2. Peel potatoes, cut into very small dices and leave them in water.
3. Cut cabbage into very small dices.
4. Wash, remove the eye of the tomato and make a small incision at the bottom. Boil water and blanch the tomatoes for one to two minutes and remove immediately.
5. Peel, deseed and puree or mince the tomatoes.
6. Peel onion and garlic and chop as finely as possible. Wash and chop celery and basil leaves, reserve a few basil leaves for garnish.
7. Heat olive oil in a pan, add onion and garlic and sauté till they turn translucent.
8. Add celery, carrot and potato pieces. Stir continuously and cook for five minutes.
9. Add cabbage, tomatoes and cook stirring continuously. Add salt, white pepper powder, basil and the macaroni, stir and add stock or water and bring it to a boil.
10. Lower the flame and simmer till the vegetables are cooked and the soup has thickened.
11. Crush the remaining basil with a pestle and garnish the soup.

NUTRITIONAL INFORMATION

Calories	125
Proteins	1.8
Fat	2.3
Carbohydrates	14.0
Fibre	1.0

*Exotic sweet basil comes from the same family as tulsi. Tulsi is worshipped in India. **Tulsi** is used to treat fever, colds, flue, stomach cramps, vomiting, headaches and menstrual cramps. Its role in reducing cholesterol and triglycerides is also worth mentioning.*

T I P   *Basil is known to emit ozone rather than oxygen that is emitted by other plants.*

CELESTIAL VEGETABLE SOUP

INGREDIENTS

Button mushrooms 8-10
Carrot .... 1 medium sized
Capsicum .... 1 medium sized
Shelled green peas .... ½ cup
Vegetable stock or water ..... 3 cups
Corn flour .... 2 tblspns

Egg white (optional) .... of 1 egg
Oil .... 1 tspn
Sweet corn niblets .... 2 tblspns
Salt .... to taste
Sugar .... a pinch
Red chillies whole (crushed) ..... ½ tspn

METHOD OF PREPARATION

1. Wash and cut mushrooms into four. Peel and cut carrots into one fourth inch pieces. Wash capsicum, halve, deseed and cut into one fourth inch pieces
2. Boil carrots and green peas in vegetable stock or water. Keep aside.
3. Dissolve corn flour in half a cup of water. Beat egg white (if using) lightly. Keep aside.
4. Heat oil, add capsicum and mushroom pieces and cook for two to three minutes on high heat.
5. Add warm vegetable stock or water along with carrots, green peas and sweet corn niblets. Bring it to a boil. Add salt to taste, sugar and crushed red chillies.
6. Stir in corn flour dissolved in water, stirring continuously. Cook at boiling hot temperature for one minute.
7. Finally add the beaten egg white in a thin stream (if using), stir lightly and serve hot.

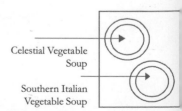

Celestial Vegetable Soup

Southern Italian Vegetable Soup

T I P *If you are using whole fresh peas, do not throw away the peel. Instead use them as vegetable after removing and discarding thin inner layer.*

CREAMED RED PUMPKIN AND APPLE

INGREDIENTS

Red pumpkin .... 250 gms	Skimmed milk .... 1 cup
Apples 2	Lemon juice .... 2 tspns
Onion........................... 1 large sized	Curry powder .... 2 tspns
Oil .... 2 tspns	Salt .... to taste
Bay leaves 2	Pepper powder .... ½ tspn
Vegetable stock .... 1 ½ cups	Parsley .... a few sprigs

METHOD OF PREPARATION

1. Peel, wash and grate the red pumpkin.
2. Wash, core and roughly chop the apples. Peel and roughly chop the onion.
3. Heat oil in a pan, add bay leaves followed by chopped onion and saute till translucent.
4. Add grated pumpkin and chopped apples. Cook on high heat for a couple of minutes stirring continuously.
5. Add half the stock and cook the vegetables until soft.
6. Cool the vegetables, remove the bay leaves and puree cooked vegetables in a mixer.
7. Heat pureed vegetables and add the remaining stock and milk. Mix well and bring it to a boil.
8. Add lemon juice, curry powder, salt and pepper powder.
9. Garnish with parsley and serve hot.

NUTRITIONAL INFORMATION

Calories	70
Proteins	2.4
Fat	2.3
Carbohydrates	11.4
Fibre	0.9

Red pumpkin is a vegetable fruit that is low in calories (25 cals/100 gms). The deeper the yellow orange colour the more betacarotene it has. It is alkaline in nature and can be taken when one has acidity.

It is easily digested and can be given to the sick or even to children.

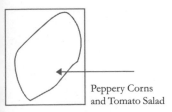

Peppery Corns
and Tomato Salad

CYPRUS TOMATO SOUP

INGREDIENTS

Ripe tomatoes ... 7 - 8 medium sized
Onion .... 1 medium sized
Garlic .... 5-6 cloves
Celery .... 1 stick
Fresh parsley .... a few sprigs
Olive oil .... 1 tblspn

Bay leaf 1
Vegetable stock .... 2 cups
Shell pasta .... ½ cup
Salt .... to taste
Pepper powder .... ½ tspn

METHOD OF PREPARATION

1. Wash and roughly chop the tomatoes. Peel and finely chop onion and garlic.
2. Wash and finely chop celery and parsley.
3. Heat olive oil gently in a pan, add onion, celery, garlic and bay leaf and sauté for a while.
4. Add the chopped tomatoes and one cup water and stir. Cook on high heat till it starts boiling.
5. Reduce heat, cover and cook on low heat for fifteen to twenty minutes, stirring occasionally, until very soft. Strain and keep the liquid aside.
6. Cool the cooked tomatoes and puree them in a mixer. Stir in the reserved tomato liquid.
7. Heat the pureed tomato mixture in a pan, add the remaining vegetable stock and bring it to a boil.
8. Add pasta, cover and simmer till the pasta is cooked. Add salt and pepper.
9. Garnish with chopped parsley and serve hot.

CURRIED CAULIFLOWER SOUP

INGREDIENTS

Cauliflower .... 1 medium sized	Cumin seeds .... ½ tspn
Potato .... 1 medium sized	Mustard seeds .... ¼ tspn
Onion .... 1 medium sized	Turmeric powder .... ½ tspn
Garlic .... 4 cloves	Coriander powder .... 2 tspns
Ginger .... ½ inch knob	Skimmed milk yogurt .... 1 cup
Fresh coriander leaves ... a few sprigs	Skimmed milk .... ½ cup
Refined oil .... 1 ½ tspns	Bengal gram flour (Besan) ... 2 tspns
Vegetable stock .... 4 cups	Salt .... to taste

METHOD OF PREPARATION

NUTRITIONAL INFORMATION

Calories	140
Proteins	5.8
Fat	5.1
Carbohydrates	16.3
Fibre	0.7

Leaves, seeds and oil of **mustard** *plant have medicinal value. Mustard is largely used as a digestive condiment and is good for sore throat, congestion and muscular pain. Black mustard is more pungent than yellow or white mustard.*

1. Wash and cut the cauliflower into small florets and keep it in salted water.
2. Wash, peel and roughly cut the potato into small pieces and keep them in water.
3. Peel and finely chop onion, garlic and ginger. Clean, wash and chop the fresh coriander leaves.
4. Heat oil in a thick-bottomed pan, add chopped onions and sauté for two minutes. Add chopped ginger and garlic and sauté for a further two minutes. Drain and add the chopped potatoes.
5. Drain and add the cauliflower florets and stir on high heat for three to four minutes.
6. Stir in two cups of vegetable stock and bring to a boil. Cover and simmer for sometime till cauliflower and potatoes are cooked.
7. Once cooked, remove from heat and cool the mixture. Puree the cauliflower and potato mixture in a blender.
8. Heat oil, add cumin seeds and mustard seeds. When they start to crackle, add the cauliflower and potato puree along with the remaining vegetable stock. Mix well and let it simmer. Add turmeric and coriander powders and mix well.
9. In a bowl whisk skimmed milk yogurt with skimmed milk. Add Bengal gram flour (besan) and continue to whisk so that there are no lumps. Stir it in the soup and cook for a while.
10. Season it with salt.
11. Serve hot garnished with chopped coriander leaves.

T I P *A leftover dish made of potatoes and cauliflower can be pureed and used to make the above soup.*

CHILLED CUCUMBER AND BUTTERMILK SOUP

INGREDIENTS

Cucumber .... 2 medium sized
Ginger .... ½ inch knob
Green chilli 1
Mint leaves .... a few sprigs
Lemon juice .... 2 tspns
Buttermilk .... 2 cups
Salt .... to taste
Pepper powder .... ½ tspn

METHOD OF PREPARATION

1. Peel and wash the cucumber. Deseed and roughly chop.
2. Peel, wash and roughly chop ginger. Wash, deseed and chop the green chilli.
3. Clean and wash the mint leaves. Reserve a few sprigs for garnish and finely chop the rest.
4. Put cucumber, ginger, green chilli and lemon juice in a blender and blend till smooth.
5. Stir in buttermilk and chopped mint leaves. Season it with salt and freshly ground pepper powder.
6. Garnish with mint leaves and serve chilled.

T I P *Buttermilk should be lump free. If you do not have buttermilk, you can mix equal quantities of curd and water and whisk till smooth.*

FRENCH ONION AND GARLIC SOUP

INGREDIENTS

Onions .... 3 medium sized	Cheese .... ¼ cup
Garlic .... 6 cloves	Vegetable stock .... 4 cups
Carrot .... 1 medium sized	Salt .... to taste
Brown bread .... 4 slices	White pepper powder .... ¼ tspn
Olive oil .... 1 tblspn	

METHOD OF PREPARATION

1. Peel and slice onions. Peel and chop five cloves of garlic.
2. Wash, peel and cut carrot into two, lengthwise. Make thin slices.
3. Cut the brown bread into small roundels, toast it with olive oil and rub with the remaining garlic clove. Grate cheese and keep aside.
4. In a thick-bottomed pan, heat oil and sauté sliced onions till brown. Keep aside a few slices of crisply fried brown onions for garnishing. Add chopped garlic and sauté.
5. Add sliced carrots and sauté for a few minutes.
6. Add vegetable stock and bring it to boil. Reduce heat and let it simmer for ten to fifteen minutes.
7. Add salt and white pepper powder.
8. To serve, ladle soup into individual bowls, float the toasted brown bread, top it with grated cheese and fried brown onions and serve hot.

NUTRITIONAL INFORMATION

Calories	195
Proteins	6.7
Fat	7.5
Carbohydrates	24.7
Fibre	0.9

Cheese is a valuable food because it is mainly protein, has high amounts of calcium and vitamin A. Moreover cheese is even fortified with Vitamin D. Cheddar cheese contains about 25% protein, 32% fat and 2% milk sugar (lactose). Use homemade low fat paneer as a substitute for processed cheese which is high in calories, fats and sodium.

T I P *Since the quantity of oil used for frying onions is minimal, sliced onions would not become crisp as in the case of traditional French onion soup. However, if available, use dehydrated sliced onions as they stay crisp.*

CHILLED MUST! MELON SOUP

INGREDIENTS

Musk Melon .... 1 (approx. 1 kg.)	Lemon juice .... 3 tblspns
Ginger .... 1 one inch knob	Crushed ice .... 2 cups
Mint leaves .... a few sprigs	Salt .... to taste
Skimmed milk yogurt .... ¼ cup	Pepper powder .... ¼ tspn

METHOD OF PREPARATION

1. Cut the musk melon into two, remove and discard seeds. Peel and cut into one inch sized pieces.
2. Peel ginger, wash well and cut it roughly. Wash the mint leaves thoroughly. Reserve a sprig for garnishing.
3. In a blender or a food processor, puree musk melon along with ginger and mint leaves. Add yogurt, lemon juice and crushed ice; blend for a few minutes more.
4. Season with salt and pepper powder.
5. Serve chilled garnished with a sprig of mint.

T I P
1. *Consistency of this soup is normally very thick, however, if you prefer you may dilute it by adding half a cup of chilled skimmed milk.*
2. *Go easy on mint leaves as too much mint flavour and taste can be overpowering.*

SNACKS

A snack can be simply defined as a light food, something that is eaten in-between regular meals. Sometimes they also serve as a substitute for a meal, more so for people who keep busy schedules which allow little time for full meals. With changing lifestyles 'fast food' (which is also a kind of snack) has established its foothold in our daily diets.

Quite often these snacks are high in sugar, salt and fat but fall short when it comes to the essential nutrient content and this is definitely a cause for concern. However these very snacks can be made healthy with proper use of ingredients and cooking methods.

Here are some tips to make simple yet nutritionally rich low calorie snacks:

❖ Instead of fried snacks use steamed and boiled ones that can be enjoyed by all specially those with cardiovascular diseases, diabetes and those who are on a fat restricted diet.

❖ With thoughtful use of pulses, lentils and tofu vegetarian snacks can be made rich in protein content.

❖ Addition of *paneer* (made from skimmed milk), to sandwich toppings and cutlets etc. will improve the protein content.

❖ Instead of using only potatoes as the base for cutlets, add vegetables like carrots or green leafy vegetables (spinach, *methi*), thus increasing the vitamin and mineral content.

❖ Instead of frying, roast some ingredients like peanuts, *chana dal, chivda,* etc.

❖ Serve snacks with freshly made chutneys from mint and coriander leaves instead of readymade sauces which use preservatives and are high in sodium that can prove harmful to health. Mint and coriander chutneys on the other hand are rich in vitamin C, iron, Beta-carotene, calcium and B complex.

❖ Instead of using refined flour use whole meal flour along with bran. This will help increase the fibre content.

APPLE AND CHEESE TOAST

INGREDIENTS

Apples .... 2 large sized		Whole wheat bread .... 4 slices
Lemon juice .... 1 tblspn		Low-fat cottage cheese ..... 120 gms
Cashew nuts 8		Cinnamon powder .... ½ tspn
Orange juice .... ½ cup		Honey .... 1 tblspn

METHOD OF PREPARATION

1. Peel, core and cut the apples into thick slices. Sprinkle lemon juice on apple slices.
2. Toast the cashew nuts in a pan or in a preheated oven till light golden, cool and crush coarsely.
3. Heat a non-stick pan and gently poach the apple slices in the orange juice for about ten minutes or until just soft, turn them over carefully for even cooking.
4. Toast the bread slices, trim the sides.
5. Grate the cottage cheese and mix with the crushed cashew nuts thoroughly.
6. Spread this mixture on the toasted bread slice and arrange the cooked apple slices on top.
7. Sprinkle cinnamon powder and place under a hot grill or in a preheated oven (180 degree Celsius) until browned to light golden.
8. Drizzle the honey on the hot toasts, cut to desired shape and serve.

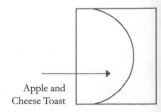

Apple and Cheese Toast

HEALTHY PIZZA

INGREDIENTS

For pizza base
Dried yeast .... 1 ½ tspns
Sugar .... 1 tspn
Whole meal flour .... 1 ½ cups
Soya flour .... 2 tblspns
Salt .... 1 tspn
Olive oil .... 1 tblspn
Wheat bran .... 2 tblspns
For Sauce
Tomatoes .... 4 medium sized
Onion .... 1 small sized
Garlic .... 4-5 cloves

Fresh basil .... a few leaves
Olive oil .... 2 tblspns
Salt .... to taste
Crushed dried red chillies .... 1 tspn
For Topping
Mushrooms 10-12
Capsicum .... 1 medium sized
Tomatoes .... 2 medium sized
Onion .... 1 medium sized
Low fat mozzarella cheese ... 1 tblspn
Oregano (dried) .... ¼ tspn

METHOD OF PREPARATION

1. Mix yeast with sugar and one teaspoon warm water and leave aside until frothy.
2. Add frothy yeast to a mixture of whole meal and soya flour. Add salt, olive oil and wheat bran. Add water and knead into soft dough.
3. Leave the dough covered with a damp cloth in a warm place for about forty five minutes or until the dough is about double in volume.
4. Divide pizza dough into four, roll out each portion into medium thick eight inch discs. Prick them with a fork all over. Pre-heat an oven to 220 degree Celsius.
5. For the sauce, wash and chop tomatoes finely. Peel and chop onion and garlic. Wash and tear basil leaves into small pieces. Heat olive oil in a pan, add chopped onion and garlic, stir-fry briefly and add chopped tomatoes. Add one cup of water and bring it to a boil. Stir in the basil leaves, salt and crushed dried red chillies. Simmer for about five minutes on medium heat or till it reaches thick dropping consistency.
6. For pizza topping, wash mushrooms thoroughly with plenty of water, pat them dry and slice. Wash capsicum, halve to deseed and then cut into thin strips. Wash and cut tomatoes into quarters and cut into thin strips. Peel and slice onion. Grate low-fat mozzarella cheese.
7. Spread prepared pizza sauce on rolled pizza base, top it with sliced

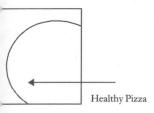

Healthy Pizza

Healthy Pizza	
Calories	100-125
Proteins	4.0
Fat	2.2
Carbohydrates	15.0
Fibre	1.0
Regular Pizza	
Calories	175-200
Proteins	4.0
Fat	6.0
Carbohydrates	28.0
Fibre	0.2

The regular pizzas that we eat have the base made up of refined flour (maida). This supplies more calories with very few other nutrients. This pizza cannot be recommended for weight watchers or diabetics. In contrast to this, the base in this recipe is made from whole wheat flour and soya flour, to which bran is also added. Compared to maida, whole-wheat flour or atta has more thiamin, riboflavin, niacin and iron. Soya flour gives us a good amount of protein. Addition of wheat bran not only increases fibre but also adds to the nutritional value of the whole dish.

Also note the use of low-fat cheese in the recipe.

onion, sliced mushrooms, tomato and capsicum strips. Finally sprinkl[e] grated low-fat mozzarella cheese to evenly cover the pizza top. Crus[h] dried oregano leaves and spronkle on the pizza.

8. Place it on greased ovenproof tray and bake in a preheated oven fo[r] about 20 minutes or until the pizza base is crisp and the cheese melts an[d] starts bubbling.

9. Remove from oven, cut into six or eight pieces and serve hot.

T I P *The pizza base can be baked in advance separately and then baked again with the topping on it at the time of consumption.*

CHATPATI TIKKI

INGREDIENTS

Raw bananas .... 2 medium sized	Roasted peanuts without skin .... ½ cup
Carrots .... 2 medium sized	Oil .... 1 tspn
Onion..................... 1 medium sized	Mustard seeds .... ½ tspn
Ginger .... 1 one inch knob	*Urad dal* .... ½ tspn
Green chillies 3-4	Red chilli powder .... 1 tspn
Mint leaves 8-10	*Chaat masala* powder .... 2 tspns
Raisins (*kishmish*) 15-20	Salt .... to taste
Seedless dates 6	Lemon juice .... 2 tspns

METHOD OF PREPARATION

1. Boil whole raw bananas in sufficient water for fifteen to twenty minutes. Cool, peel and mash well. Wash, peel and grate the carrots. Peel and finely chop onion and ginger.

2. Wash, remove stem and finely chop green chillies. Wash and finely chop mint leaves.

3. Wash raisins and roughly chop them with seedless dates. Divide this into twelve equal portions. Grind roasted peanuts to a coarse powder.

4. Heat oil in a non-stick pan and add mustard seeds, let them crackle and add *urad dal*. Let it cook till it starts turning brown. Add chopped onion, ginger, garlic and green chillies. Stir-fry for half a minute. Add red chilli powder, mix and quickly add grated carrot.

5. Cook over medium heat for two to three minutes. Sprinkle chopped mint leaves, *chaat masala* powder, mix well and remove from heat.

6. Cool and mix the cooked masala with the mashed raw bananas. Add salt to taste, lemon juice and mix well.

7. Divide this mixture into twelve equal portions. Stuff a portion of the date and raisin mixture into each portion of raw banana mixture.

8. Wet your palm and form this mixture into a patty (*tikki*) of not more than half inch thickness.

9. Coat the *tikkis* with coarse peanut powder, pressing them lightly with your palms.

10. Heat a non-stick fry pan or a griddle plate (*tawa*), place the peanut coated *tikkis*. Cook on medium heat till the crust is crisp and nicely brown. Make sure that the *tikkis* are heated through. Serve immediately with a tangy sauce of your choice.

NUTRITIONAL INFORMATION

Calories	160
Proteins	4.5
Fat	5.9
Carbohydrates	22.5
Fibre	1.6

Raisins are dried grapes and are a good source of glucose, iron and phosphorous. Phosphorous is an important component of the nerve cells and plays a central role in energy metabolism. Raisins are an excellent natural laxative.

SPICED EGGPLANT SAVOURY

INGREDIENTS

Eggplant (brinjal) .... 1 medium sized (approx. 250 gms)

Garlic .... 5 cloves

Tomatoes .... 3 medium sized

Onion..................... 1 medium sized

Green chillies 2-3

Mint leaves .... ¼ cup

Fresh coriander leaves .... ¼ cup

Lemon juice .... 1 tspn

Salt .... to taste

Oil .... 1 tspn

Brown bread .... 4 slices

METHOD OF PREPARATION

1. Wash eggplant, prick it using a fork.
2. Roast eggplant over direct flame or in a pre heated oven until soft. Cool roasted eggplant, then remove the outer burnt skin completely. Wash it well. Drain excess water and chop it fine.
3. Peel and chop garlic. Wash and chop tomatoes. Peel and chop onion. Wash green chillies, remove stem and then chop. Clean, wash mint and fresh coriander leaves and chop them finely.
4. Mix chopped eggplants with chopped onion, chopped tomatoes, chopped garlic, chopped green chillies, chopped fresh coriander leaves, lemon juice and salt.
5. Cook this mixture in a non-stick pan with a little oil on medium heat until it dries well.
6. Toast brown bread slices till crisp. Spread this mixture on the toasted bread pieces. Sprinkle chopped mint leaves on top, cut each slice in two or four pieces. Serve warm, chilled or at room temperature.

NUTRITIONAL INFORMATION

Calories	90
Proteins	3.5
Fat	1.6
Carbohydrates	17.0
Fibre	1.5

Eggplant or brinjal is a low calorie vegetable and a good source of phosphorous and iron. It has a fair amount of riboflavin, folic acid, choline and potassium.

 T I P *To make it more delicious, grated low-fat mozzarella can be put on top and then put in hot oven until cheese melts and starts bubbling.*

SPINACH AND MUSHROOM PANCAKES

INGREDIENTS

Spinach leaves ... 2 medium bundles	Salt .... to taste
Onion .... 1 medium sized	White pepper powder .... ¼ tspn
Garlic .... 6-8 cloves	Whole wheat flour (*Atta*) .... ¾ cup
Fresh mushrooms .... 100 gms	Skimmed milk .... ¾ cup
Oil .... 1 tspn	Carom seeds (*Ajwain*) .... ¼ tspn

METHOD OF PREPARATION

1. Clean and wash the spinach leaves thoroughly. Drain and chop roughly.
2. Peel and chop onion. Peel and chop garlic. Wash and wipe mushrooms with a kitchen towel and chop them.
3. Heat oil in a pan, add chopped garlic, stir-fry briefly. Add chopped onion and mushrooms and cook till onions become soft and translucent. Cook on high heat so that the excess moisture from onions and mushrooms dries to some extent.
4. Add chopped spinach, add salt and white pepper powder, and then cook spinach until all the moisture evaporates. Remove from fire and divide the spinach mixture into eight equal portions and keep warm.
5. Mix salt with whole wheat flour and add milk. Whisk well. Add water as required, to make a smooth batter of pouring consistency. Strain the batter if there are lumps.
6. Mix in the *ajwain* and stir well. Rest the batter for at least fifteen minutes.
7. Heat a six inch non-stick pan. Grease with a little oil, if required. Pour half a ladle of batter and spread into a round shape. Cook for half a minute on medium heat, turn over and cook slightly.
8. Spread a portion of cooked spinach on three fourth portion of the pancake and then roll it ensuring that the filling does not spill out.
9. Cook rest of the pancakes in similar way. Serve immediately.

NUTRITIONAL INFORMATION

Calories	150
Proteins	7.0
Fat	2.3
Carbohydrates	25.4
Fibre	1.3

Mushrooms have a lot of health benefits. They are a perfect alternative to meat not only because of their rich and succulent taste, but they are also low in calories, fat and are cholesterol free, rich in vitamins and minerals.

Some types of mushrooms are rich in protein, fibre, Vitamin B complex and minerals like calcium, magnesium, potassium, phosphorous and zinc.

Research in Japan confirms that mushroom lowers serum cholesterol and treats blood pressure, chronic fatigue and infection in general.

T I P *The pancakes can be topped with a little low fat cheese and gratinated in a grill just before serving.*

HOT AND SOUR IDLIS

INGREDIENTS

Pigeon pea split (*Arhar dal*) ... 1 cup
Rice .... 1 cup
Red chillies whole 6
Tamarind pulp .... 2 tblspns
Jaggery (grated) .... 1 tblspn

Asafoetida .... one large pinch
Turmeric powder .... ½ tspn
Salt .... to taste
Onions .... 2 small sized

METHOD OF PREPARATION

1. Pick, wash and soak the *dal* and the rice separately in three cups of water for four to six hours. Drain and keep aside. Do not mix. Grind the red chillies and tamarind to a fine paste.
2. Grind dal smoothly and rice coarsely separately. Mix them thoroughly.
3. Add the paste of red chillies and tamarind, grated jaggery, asafoetida, turmeric powder and salt and mix well. Leave it aside for four to five hours to ferment.
4. Peel, wash and finely chop onions.
5. Grease the *idli* moulds. Heat a little water in a steam pot.
6. Pour the batter into the moulds, sprinkle the chopped onions on top and steam for about fifteen to twenty minutes or till done.
7. Serve hot with a chutney of your choice.

T
I
P
Though these idlis are quite different from traditional idlis made from rice and urad dal, they are equally tasty. As these idlis have tamarind, chillies and jaggery, you can eat them as an any time snack.

FRENCH BREAD CRISPIES

INGREDIENTS

Whole meal French bread/loaf.... 1
Olive oil .... 2 tblspns
Tomatoes .... 3 large
Garlic .... 5–6 cloves
Fresh basil .... a few leaves

Salt .... to taste
Crushed pepper corns .... 1 tspn
Red chilli flakes .... ½ tspn
Dry oregano .... a pinch

METHOD OF PREPARATION

1. Cut whole meal French loaf diagonally into half inch thick slices. Wash and finely chop tomatoes. Peel and chop garlic.
2. Clean and wash fresh basil leaves. Chop half of the leaves and cut the remaining leaves into thin strips and keep them in cold water.
3. Apply a little olive oil on the bread slices and toast in a preheated oven or salamander till they become slightly crisp.
4. Mix the chopped tomatoes with garlic, chopped basil and remaining olive oil.
5. Season it with salt, crushed pepper corns, chilli flakes and dry oregano. Mix it thoroughly.
6. Spread this mixture on the toasted brown bread and transfer it once again to the preheated oven or salamander. Cook till bread starts to become golden brown at the edges.
7. Serve immediately garnished with fresh basil strips.

NUTRITIONAL INFORMATION

Per Piece	
Calories	75
Proteins	2.1
Fat	2.3
Carbohydrates	11.8
Fibre	0.4

Croutons, papries *used for* chats *&* bhels *are all under the category of* **crispies**. *These conventionally fried crispies can add a lot of unwanted fat and calories. To avoid this use roasted or toasted items to give a healthy alternative to fried crispies.*

CHILLI TACOS

INGREDIENTS

Lettuce, preferably iceberg .... ½ bunch
Spring onions 2
Green chillies 2
Mint leaves .... a few sprigs
Cherry tomatoes 8
Low fat cheese .... ½ cup
Cheddar cheese .... ½ cup

Taco shells 8
Baked beans in tomato sauce ..... 1 cup
Chilli sauce .... 2 tspns
Lemon juice .... 2 tblspns
Salt .... to taste
Pepper powder .... ½ tspn

NUTRITIONAL INFORMATION

Per Piece	
Calories	160
Proteins	6.1
Fat	9.5
Carbohydrates	13.5
Fibre	0.9

*Home cooked **Mexican food** is considered as healthy because it has a right blend of cereals, beans and vegetables. Basic foodstuffs used in Mexican cooking are maize/maize flour, beans, chillies and tomatoes. Because it is simple to prepare and has a lot of health appeal, Mexican cooking is gaining popularity globally.*

METHOD OF PREPARATION

1. Wash the lettuce well under running water and shred. Peel and chop the onions. Wash, slit into two, deseed and finely chop green chillies. Clean, wash and chop half the mint leaves keeping aside the rest for garnish.
2. Wash and quarter the cherry tomatoes. Grate the low fat cheese and cheddar cheese separately.
3. Warm the taco shells in a preheated oven for a few minutes.
4. In a bowl take the baked beans and add grated low fat cheese, chopped onions, chilli sauce, lemon juice and chopped mint leaves. Add salt and pepper powder, mix lightly.
5. Fill the taco shells with shredded lettuce leaves spread evenly and then with the baked beans mixture till the shells are about three fourth full.
6. Top the shells with grated cheddar cheese, quartered cherry tomatoes and a sprig of mint.
7. Serve immediately.

T I P *Though the taco shells are fried, as the quantity of salad used is more, it becomes a healthy meal with controlled calories.*

RED COLESLAW IN PITA POCKETS

INGREDIENTS

Red cabbage......... ½ medium sized	Low fat cheese spread..... 3 tblspns
Onions .... 2 small sized	Skimmed milk yogurt ...... 3 tblspns
Red radish 2	Salt .... to taste
Red apples .... 2 medium sized	Pepper powder .... ½ tspn
Lemon juice .... 1 tblspn	Pita bread............... 4 medium sized

METHOD OF PREPARATION

1. Wash and shred cabbage. Peel and thinly slice onions and radish.
2. Peel, core and grate the apples. Mix the sliced vegetables, grated apple and lemon juice together in a bowl.
3. Add the cheese spread, skimmed milk yogurt, salt and pepper and mix well. Divide the red coleslaw into eight equal portions.
4. Warm the pita bread on a griddle plate or a preheated oven. Cut each pita bread into two and fill each half with a portion of red coleslaw.
5. Serve with a sauce or chutney of your choice.

NUTRITIONAL INFORMATION

Per Piece	
Calories	120
Proteins	4.4
Fat	1.6
Carbohydrates	24.4
Fibre	0.6

Red Cabbage is chiefly valued for its high mineral and vitamin content and alkaline salts. Moreover 100 gms supplies only 27 calories. It is well digested even if uncooked and hence taken raw in form of salad.

Recent research has identified a valuable content called 'tartonic acid', which inhibits the conversion of sugar and other carbohydrates to fat. This probably justifies the role of cabbage in slimmer's diet.

PIQUANT POTATOES IN JACKETS

INGREDIENTS

Potatoes .... 4 large sized
Onion........................... 1 small sized
Ginger................. 1 one inch knob
Garlic .... 3-4 cloves
Coriander leaves .... a few sprigs
Oil............................... 1 tblspn
Cumin seeds .... 1 tspn

Coriander powder .... 2 tspns
Turmeric powder .... ½ tspn
Garlic salt............................... 1 tspn
Pepper powder .... ½ tspn
Salt .... to taste
Yogurt .... 1 cup

NUTRITIONAL INFORMATION

Calories	140
Proteins	3.3
Fat	2.2
Carbohydrates	27.9
Fibre	0.8

We all agree that it is not just important to cook well, but also to present the cooked food in an appealing way to stimulate appetite and give a sense of satisfaction after eating.

It is very important to choose the right garnish for the right food. Garnishes like cream, butter, nuts, cheese are high in calories and can add considerable amount of calories to a dish. On the other hand coriander, parsley, grated carrot, tomatoes, lemon rind, orange peel are examples of almost zero calorie but eye appealing garnishes.

METHOD OF PREPARATION

1. Wash and prick the potatoes with a fork and bake in a preheated oven at 190 degree Celsius for forty minutes or till done.
2. Cut the potatoes in half and scoop out the flesh without spoiling the skin. Skin of the potato is popularly known as the jacket.
3. Peel and finely chop onions. Peel and finely chop ginger and garlic. Wash and chop the coriander leaves.
4. Heat oil in a pan. Add cumin seeds, chopped onion, ginger and garlic. Sauté for a minute.
5. Add the scooped potatoes, coriander powder, turmeric powder, garlic salt and pepper powder.
6. Cook further on medium heat for two minutes, stirring occasionally. Cool slightly and mix in half cup of well beaten yogurt.
7. Spoon the mixture back into the potato jackets and top each with a tablespoonful of remaining yogurt. Garnish with chopped coriander and serve hot.

MUSHROOM AND PANEER KABAB

INGREDIENTS

Button mushrooms 14-16	Oil .... 2 tspns
Cottage cheese (*Paneer*) ..... 200 gms	Red chilli flakes .... 1 tspn
Onions .... 3 medium sized	Honey....................................... 2 tspns
Capsicum .... 2 large sized	Cumin powder .... 1 tspn
Cherry tomatoes 18-20	*Garam masala* powder .... 1 tspn
Green chillies 2-3	Salt .... to taste
Ginger .... 1 two inches knob	Lemon juice .... 2 tspns
Garlic .... 8-10 cloves	*Chaat masala* .... 1 tspn

METHOD OF PREPARATION

1. Clean mushrooms. Cut the *paneer* into one and half inches sized cubes. Peel, wash and cut onions into one inch sized chunks. Wash, halve, remove seeds and cut capsicum into one inch sized pieces. Wash cherry tomatoes.
2. Wash, deseed and roughly chop the green chillies. Peel ginger and garlic and grind them to a paste along with green chillies.
3. In a bowl mix together oil, ginger-garlic and green chilli paste, red chilli flakes, honey, cumin powder, *garam masala* powder, salt, lemon juice, and *chaat masala*.
4. Marinate the cottage cheese, button mushrooms, cherry tomatoes, capsicum and onion chunks in this mixture for about an hour.
5. Take eight inches long wooden satay sticks or skewers and soak them in water for half an hour. Remove from water and thread marinated *paneer* cubes, mushrooms, cherry tomatoes, capsicum and onion pieces one after the other on the sticks or skewers.
6. Cook on an open charcoal fire or directly over gas flame for five minutes, rotating the stick for even cooking. Alternatively cook in a preheated oven (180 degrees Celsius) for about fifteen minutes.

NUTRITIONAL INFORMATION

Calories	155
Proteins	8.2
Fat	9.5
Carbohydrates	12
Fibre	0.8

When we cook foods we use some **garam masala** *which actually gives the spicy aromatic flavour and taste to food. If used in small quantities it can stimulate the secretion of digestive juices, which can aid digestion.*

STUFFED CHILLIES

INGREDIENTS

Large green chillies 12-16	Cumin powder .... ½ tspn
Onion...................... 1 medium sized	Red chilli powder .... ½ tspn
Spinach .... ½ bunch	Salt .... to taste
Fresh mushrooms .... ½ cup	Bread crumbs .... ¼ cup
Processed cheese.................. 50 gms	Oil ...... for greasing the baking dish
Oil.. 1 tspn	

METHOD OF PREPARATION

1. Wash and slit the green chillies carefully only on one side, remove seeds and keep aside. Peel and finely chop the onion.
2. Wash the spinach thoroughly under running water. Remove stems, blanch in boiling water for a minute and take out immediately. Refresh in cold water, drain and chop the blanched spinach.
3. Wash and chop the mushrooms. Grate cheese and keep it aside.
4. Heat oil in a pan on medium heat, add chopped onions and cook, stirring continuously till onions turn light golden brown. Add the chopped mushrooms and cook for another two to three minutes, stirring frequently.
5. Add the blanched spinach and cook for another two minutes. Add cumin powder, red chilli powder and salt. Mix well.
6. Remove from heat and cool. Add breadcrumbs and grated cheese to the mixture.
7. Stuff the green chillies with the spinach and mushroom mixture and bake in a preheated oven at 200 degrees Celsius for about twenty minutes or until the chillies are softened.
8. Serve hot.

VEGETABLES

Vegetables are perhaps the most versatile of all natural food items. In fact they are Nature's best gift to mankind and are an essential part of our diet. Their natural taste and flavours not only add to the palatability of a meal but also add enormously to the nutritional value by contributing some of the important nutrients like vitamins, minerals and fibre. Besides, vegetables play a key role in neutralizing the acid produced during digestion of protein-rich and fatty foods and provide a large amount of roughage, which promotes digestion and helps in preventing constipation.

Vegetables can be broadly classified under roots and tubers, leafy vegetables and other vegetables. Potatoes, tapioca, sweet potatoes, yam, etc. are rich in carbohydrates whereas peas and beans are a good sources of proteins. All dark, green, leafy vegetables are rich in Beta-carotene, Vitamin C and minerals like iron, calcium , potassium, magnesium, etc. Peas, broad beans, tomatoes (ripe), garlic and greens provide vitamin B complex. Since there is very little carbohydrate or fat present in vegetables, they contribute very little to the caloric value of the food to which they are added. The daily requirements of some of the essential nutrients like vitamins and minerals can be met very well by consuming forty to hundred grams of green leafy vegetables and sixty to hundred grams of other vegetables [as suggested by the Indian Council Of Medical Research (ICMR) committee on Recommended Dietary Allowances (RDA)].

Though India is one of largest producers of vegetables worldwide, extensive studies show that the consumption is much lower than the recommended allowance. Hence there is a need to encourage each member of the family to eat vegetables in plenty. As it is Indian cuisine doesn't lack in vegetable dishes. Each state has a wide variety of dishes based on local vegetables and when added up make an impressive list to choose from.

Some healthy tips to be remembered while cooking vegetables:

❖ Wash vegetables well before cooking to get rid of any insecticide that may still be sticking to them. They should be not soaked in water but cleaned under running water. If soaked, some of the vitamins and minerals may be lost.

❖ Care should be taken to scrape or peel off as little of the vegetable as possible. This is because most of the minerals and vitamins will be present in the layers immediately below the outer skin. Vegetables such as potatoes should be cooked with the skin on. The skin can be peeled later.

❖ Vegetables should be cut into large pieces to minimize nutrient loss.

❖ Vegetables should not be overcooked as it prevents loss of important nutrients and also helps to retain the natural colour and flavour of vegetables. Do not add cooking soda to retain colour while cooking green vegetables.

❖ Any extra water left after cooking should be added to soups or other liquid preparations.

CARROT AND ONION FLORENTINE

INGREDIENTS

Fresh spinach .... 2-3 medium sized bundles
Cornflour .... 2 tblspns
Carrots .... 3-4 medium sized
Broad beans (*Papdi*) .... 100 gms
Onions .... 2 medium sized
Garlic .... 6-7 cloves
Oil .... 1 tspn
Salt .... to taste
White pepper powder .... to taste
Skimmed milk .... 2 cups
Mixed herbs (dried) .... ¼ tspn
Fresh brown bread crumbs ... ¼ cup

METHOD OF PREPARATION

1. Clean, trim and thoroughly wash the spinach under running water. Drain and finely chop the spinach. Dissolve the cornflour in quarter cup water.
2. Wash, peel and cut carrots into one and a half cm. sized cubes. Wash, string and cut broad beans into one and a half cm. sized pieces. Peel and thinly slice the onion. Peel garlic and crush them lightly.
3. Heat oil in a non-stick pan, add half the quantity of crushed garlic, stir briefly and add the chopped spinach. Sauté for four to five minutes over high heat, stirring occasionally or until the spinach is cooked completely. Add salt and white pepper powder to taste, stir well and remove from fire.
4. Heat the skimmed milk in a saucepan and bring to boil.
5. Add the remaining crushed garlic, carrots and broad beans and sliced onion. Cover and simmer for three to four minutes, stirring frequently. Add salt and white pepper powder to taste.
6. Gradually add the dissolved cornflour, stirring continuously, till it has a fairly thick sauce-like consistency. Sprinkle the mixed herb, stir well and remove from fire and keep warm.
7. Take an ovenproof glass or a ceramic dish and layer the cooked spinach. Pour the cooked vegetables along with the sauce over the spinach and level it with a spatula.
8. Sprinkle the fresh breadcrumbs on top of vegetables and bake in a preheated oven at 180 degrees Celsius for ten minutes.

SABZ BAHAR ARHAR DAL

INGREDIENTS

Pigeon pea split *(Arhar dal)*. ¾ cup
Cauliflower .... ¼ medium sized
Carrot .... 1 medium sized
French beans 6-8
Drumsticks 2
Green chillies 1-2
Ginger .... 1 one inch knob
Garlic .... 4-5 cloves

Turmeric powder .... ½ tspn
Oil .... 1½ tspns
Cumin seeds .... 1 tspn
Red chilli powder .... ½ tblspn
Coriander powder .... 1 tblspn
Tamarind pulp .... 1 tblspn
Salt .... to taste

METHOD OF PREPARATION

1. Pick *dal*, wash twice or thrice with plenty of water. Soak in one and a half cups of water for twenty minutes.
2. Trim and cut cauliflower into small florets, wash and soak in warm salted water. Peel, wash and cut carrot into one inch dices. String French beans and cut into one inch dices.
3. Wash and cut the drumsticks into two-inch pieces. Wash, remove stem and slit green chillies into two. Peel, wash and chop ginger and garlic.
4. Pressure-cook the *dal* in the same water in which it was soaked, with slit green chilies and turmeric powder, for four to five minutes or until soft.
5. Similarly cook the cauliflower, carrots, drumstick and French beans in one cup water in the pressure cooker for three to four minutes or until tender.
6. Heat oil in a non-stick pan, add cumin seeds, stir briefly and add chopped ginger, garlic and sauté for a while.
7. Add red chilli powder and coriander powder and stir briefly. Dilute the tamarind pulp in quarter cup water and stir into the pan.
8. Add cooked lentils and vegetables along with its cooking liquor to the pan, mix well and add salt.
9. Continue to cook for three to four minutes on medium heat or till all the ingredients combine well and it starts bubbling. Serve hot with steamed unpolished rice.

NUTRITIONAL INFORMATION

Calories	125
Proteins	7.1
Fat	2.3
Carbohydrates	2.3
Fibre	18.6

Arhar dal (Toor dal) *is one of the most common dals used in Indian kitchens. It is high in protein (22%) and low in fat (1.7%). Arhar dal is high in phosphorous, potassium, copper, magnesium and selenium. The fresh beans of Arhar, which are used as vegetable, have high fibre content (6%). It is a good idea to add vegetables to dal preparation to increase vegetable consumption.*

MUSHROOM SOYAWADI MASALA

INGREDIENTS

NUTRITIONAL INFORMATION

Calories	150
Proteins	14.7
Fat	4.4
Carbohydrates	3.0
Fibre	0.4

Soya bean contains important nutrients like protein, complex carbohydrate, phosphorous, iron, etc. Soya bean is the only vegetable that contains complete protein. The protein quality is virtually equivalent to that of meat, milk and egg protein. Almost 40% of calories from soya bean are derived from protein, making soya bean higher in proteins than any other legumes and many animal products. Unlike many other good source of protein, soya beans are low in saturated fat and are cholesterol free. Many studies show that soya foods are helpful in fighting many types of cancer. Moreover for the past thirty years investigations have shown that consumption of soya protein selectively decreases LDL (bad cholesterol) and maintains HDL (good cholesterol).

Fresh mushrooms 15-20
Soya bean *wadi* .... 1½ cups
Ginger .... 1 one inch knob
Garlic .... 5 cloves
Onions .... 3 medium sized
Tomatoes .... 2 medium sized
Mint .... a few sprigs
Oil .... 1½ tspns

Bay leaf 1
Crushed pepper corn .... ½ tspn
Red chilli powder .... 1 tspn
Coriander powder .... 1 tspn
Turmeric powder .... ¼ tspn
Garam masala powder .... ½ tspn
Salt .... to taste

METHOD OF PREPARATION

1. Wash mushrooms in flowing water, drain well and cut into quarters.
2. Soak soya bean *wadi* in warm water for fifteen to twenty minutes. Squeeze to remove excess water, cut them into two and keep aside.
3. Peel, wash and chop ginger, garlic and onion.
4. Wash tomatoes and finely chop. Clean mint, wash thoroughly in plenty of water and finely chop.
5. Heat oil in a non-stick pan, add bay leaf, crushed pepper corn and stir-fry briefly.
6. Add chopped ginger, garlic and cook on high flame for half a minute, stirring continuously.
7. Add chopped onion and continue cooking until onion turns translucent.
8. Add red chilli powder, coriander powder and turmeric powder and stir well. Mix in the chopped tomatoes and continue cooking over medium heat.
9. Add the mushrooms and soaked soya bean *wadi*. Stir well.
10. Sprinkle *garam masala* powder, chopped mint and add salt. Mix well. Cook over high heat for two minutes. Cover and simmer over medium heat for two to three minutes.

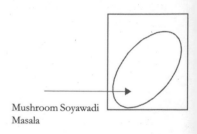

Mushroom Soyawadi Masala

KARELA ANDHRA STYLE

INGREDIENTS

Bitter gourd (*Karela*) .... 4-5 medium sized	Coriander seeds .... 1 tblspn
Salt .... to taste	Cumin seeds .... 1 tspn
Onions .... 2 medium sized	White sesame seeds .... 1 tspn
Ginger .... 1 one inch knob	Oil .... 1½ tspns
Garlic .... 5 cloves	Tomato puree .... ¼ cup
Red chillies whole 4	Grated jaggery .... 2 tblspns
	Tamarind pulp .... 2 tblspns

METHOD OF PREPARATION

1. Wash, scrape and cut *karela* in half, length wise; remove seeds and thinly slice. Apply salt and leave aside for ten to fifteen minutes. Wash with plenty of water, drain and squeeze out excess water.
2. Peel and chop onions. Peel ginger and wash well. Peel garlic. Grind ginger and garlic to a fine paste.
3. Roast whole red chillies, coriander seeds, cumin seeds and white sesame seeds on a medium hot *tawa* till light brown, stirring continuously. Cool the mixture and then grind to a fine powder.
4. Heat oil in a non-stick pan and add sliced *karela* and stir-fry for four to five minutes or till slightly browned. Add chopped onions and stir-fry for three to four minutes.
5. Add ginger and garlic paste and again stir-fry for one to two minutes.
6. Add tomato puree and cook further for a few minutes.
7. Add ground powder, grated jaggery, tamarind pulp and salt.
8. Stir well and add one cup of water and bring to a boil.
9. Reduce to medium heat, cover and simmer for five minutes.

NUTRITIONAL INFORMATION

Calories	130
Proteins	2.6
Fat	9.7
Carbohydrates	11.0
Fibre	1.7

Karela or bitter gourd is a low calorie vegetable. It has fair amount of Beta-carotene, Vitamin C and minerals like zinc. Over the years bitter gourd has been extensively studied, especially for its anti-diabetic property. Majority of work has documented its beneficial effect. The possible effect is that it stimulates enzymes, which mediate in insulin secretion which controls diabetes.

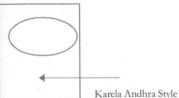

Karela Andhra Style

RATATOUILLE

INGREDIENTS

Long eggplants (Brinjal) .... 2 medium sized
Zucchini .... 2 medium sized
Salt .... to taste
Onion .... 2 medium sized
Garlic .... 4 cloves
Tomatoes .... 3 medium sized

Capsicum .... 2 medium sized
Olive oil .... 1 tblspn
Tomato puree .... 4 tblspns
Coriander powder .... ¼ tspn
Cinnamon powder .... a pinch
Basil leaves .... a few
White pepper powder .... to taste

METHOD OF PREPARATION

1. Wash and halve eggplants and zucchini lengthways. Cut them further into thick slices.
2. Place eggplants in a colander and sprinkle with salt. Top with a heavy plate and leave to degorge for one hour.
3. Peel and slice the onions into rings. Peel and chop the garlic.
4. Wash and remove eye of the tomatoes, make a cross slit on the bottom side and immerse in boiling water for half a minute.
5. Drain the tomatoes, peel, deseed and chop them roughly.
6. Cut the capsicums into halves, deseed and cut into thin strips.
7. Heat the olive oil in a non-stick pan and cook onions over low heat until translucent. Stir in the tomato puree and cook on medium heat for three to four minutes, stirring occasionally.
8. Rinse sliced eggplant and drain well. Add drained eggplant and sliced zucchini to the cooking pan.
9. Add the garlic and capsicum and simmer for about five minutes.
10. Add the blanched and chopped tomatoes, shredded basil, salt and pepper. Stir once or twice and cook over medium heat for about ten minutes, stirring frequently.
10. Adjust the seasoning and serve hot.

BEANS WITH TOMATO YOGURT SAUCE

INGREDIENTS

French beans 20-25
Spring onions .... 3 medium sized
Ginger .... 1 one inch knob
Garlic .... 5 cloves
Dried whole red chillies 2

Skimmed milk yogurt .... 1½ cups
Maize flour .... 1 tblspn
Tomatoes .... 3 medium sized
Oil .... 2 tspns
Salt .... to taste

METHOD OF PREPARATION

1. String French beans, wash them and then cut into three inch long pieces. Blanch in salted boiling water until cooked. Strain, (reserve the water to use as stock) refresh in cold water and then drain.
2. Slit the cooked beans into two and tie them up in bundles with spring onion leaves.
3. Wash, trim and finely chop spring onions. Reserve spring onion greens. Peel and wash ginger and garlic. Grind ginger and garlic to a fine paste. Crush dry whole red chillies.
4. Beat skimmed milk yogurt with maize flour.
5. Wash tomatoes, make a cross with knife and then blanch in boiling water for thirty seconds. Remove peel, deseed and then chop.
6. Heat the oil in a non-stick pan, add chopped spring onion and cook until it turns translucent.
7. Add the paste of ginger and garlic. Stir for a moment.
8. Add tomatoes and cook further for two to three minutes.
9. Reduce the heat and add beaten skimmed milk yogurt and maize flour mixture, mix well, add salt to taste, and stir continuously.
10. Warm the cooked bean bundles just before serving, in a microwave for one minute on HIGH or by briefly dipping them in boiling hot water or stock. Top with the prepared yogurt sauce.
11. Sprinkle the crushed chillies and serve hot.

NUTRITIONAL INFORMATION

Calories	115
Proteins	5.9
Fat	2.2
Carbohydrates	16.7
Fibre	4.3

Selenium, currently in news for its antioxidant properties, is also required for normal thyroid functioning. It provides immunity and prevents male infertility. But a word of caution, selenium must not be taken in excessive quantities in the form of tablets. It is naturally present in food items like onions and yogurt.

T I P *To preserve natural colour of green vegetables, cook them uncovered. Do not overcook green vegetables, and do not add any baking soda.*

59

SWEET CORN KADHI

INGREDIENTS

Green chillies 2-3
Ginger .... 1 one inch knob
Onion .... 2 medium sized
Skimmed milk yogurt .... 1 cup
Bengal gram flour (*Besan*) ... 2 tblspns
Turmeric powder .... 1 tspn
Sweet corn kernels ....
(Frozen or Tinned) .... ½ cup

Sweet corn, cream style .... ¼ cup
Salt .... to taste
Oil .... 1½ tspns
Mustard seeds .... ¼ tspn
Fennel seeds (*Saunf*) .... ½ tspn
Onion seeds (*Kalonji*) .... ¼ tspn
Dry whole red chillies 4

METHOD OF PREPARATION

1. Wash green chillies, remove stem and roughly chop.
2. Peel, wash and grind ginger to a fine paste along with the chopped green chillies. Peel and slice onion.
3. Whisk the skimmed milk yogurt with the Bengal gram flour and turmeric, thoroughly. Stir in two-cups of water and mix.
4. Pour the yogurt mixture into a thick-bottomed pan and bring it to a boil. Reduce the heat and gradually mix in the ginger and green chilli paste, sliced onion and sweet corn, cream style. Stir well and cook for two to three minutes.
5. Add the sweet corn kernels and salt to the *kadhi* and pour one cup water.
6. Simmer over medium heat for eight to ten minutes, stirring frequently or till it thickens to a curry consistency.
7. Heat oil in a small tempering pan, add mustard seeds, fennel seeds, *kalonji* and dry whole red chillies broken into two. Stir continuously and cook till they start crackling.
8. Pour this over the sweet corn *kadhi* and immediately cover with a lid to trap all the flavours and aroma.
9. Stir well and adjust salt. Serve hot with steamed unpolished rice.

T I P *While using dry or fresh corn kernels, cook in salted water till tender before adding to the kadhi.*

QUICK PRESSURE-COOKED VEGETABLES

INGREDIENTS

Carrots .... 2 medium sized	Capsicum .... 1 medium sized
Bottle Gourd (*Lauki*) .. ½ small sized	Oil .... 1 tspn
Cauliflower .... ½ small sized	Bay leaf 1
Cabbage .... ¼ small sized	Crushed pepper corn .... 1 tspn
Potato..................... 1 medium sized	Roasted cumin powder .... ½ tspn
French beans 10-12	Salt .... to taste
Tomato .... 1 medium sized	

METHOD OF PREPARATION

NUTRITIONAL
INFORMATION

1. Wash, peel and cut carrots into one and a half cm. sized pieces. Wash, peel and cut *lauki* into one and a half cm. sized pieces. Wash and separate cauliflower into small florets. Wash and cut cabbage into one and a half cm. sized pieces.

2. Wash, peel and cut potato into one and a half cm. pieces and keep them soaked in water. Wash, string and cut French beans into one and a half cm. pieces. Wash and cut tomato into eight pieces. Wash, halve, deseed and cut capsicum into one and a half cm. sized pieces.

3. Heat oil in a pressure cooker, add bay leaf and crushed pepper corn, stir-fry briefly. Add vegetables, roasted cumin powder, salt, and mix well. Stir-fry for two to three minutes.

4. Cover and cook under pressure for five to six minutes. Remove from heat.

5. Serve immediately.

Nutritional Information	
Calories	100
Proteins	2.3
Fat	4.3
Carbohydrates	15.4
Fibre	1.9

Pressure cooking not only saves time and fuel, but also retains more nutrients, colour and flavour if cooked for the right time. Pressure cooking can greatly shorten the cooking time. Shorter the cooking time, lesser the destruction of nutrients. Pressure cooking can be one of the healthy alternatives for people who like to cook with minimum oil.

SANTUNG GARDEN VEGETABLES

INGREDIENTS

Baby carrots	3-4	Oil	2 tblspns
Zucchini	4 medium sized	Star anise	1
Celery	2 stems	Five-spice powder	1 tspn
Leeks	2	Lemon juice	2 tblspns
Baby corns	6-8	Honey	1 tblspn
Snow peas or flat beans	8-10	Salt	to taste
Tofu	100 gms	Pepper powder	¼ tspn
Pineapple	2 slices	Lemon rind	½ tspn
Corn flour	1 tblspn		

NUTRITIONAL INFORMATION

Calories	190
Proteins	6.4
Fat	9.6
Carbohydrates	24.1
Fibre	2.2

Zucchini, a vegetable somewhat like turia or ridge gourd is low in calories and hence a favourite with many calorie conscious people. It contains 80-90% moisture and around 40-50 cals/100 gms.

METHOD OF PREPARATION

1. Wash, peel and cut the baby carrots into half lengthwise. Wash and cut the zucchini into thin roundels.
2. Wash and slice the celery stems and leeks. Wash the celery leaves and keep aside for garnish.
3. Wash and cut baby corns into half lengthwise. String, wash and halve the snow peas or flat beans. Cut tofu and pineapple slices into one inch sized pieces. Dissolve corn flour in quarter cup water.
4. Heat oil in a wok. Add the star anise, baby carrots, celery, leeks, snow peas and baby corn. Stir fry for about three to four minutes on high heat. Add five-spice powder. Stir. Add zucchini and stir.
5. Add tofu and pineapple; stir gently.
5. Add half cup of hot water and bring it to a boil. Stir in cornstarch dissolved in water and cook for half a minute on high heat, stirring continuously.
6. Stir in lemon juice and honey. Add salt and pepper powder.
7. Serve hot garnished with lemon rind and celery leaves.

T I P *Five-spice powder can be made at home by grinding together equal quantities of star anise, cinnamon, fennel seeds, cloves and Sichuan pepper.*

ORANGE BROCCOLI

INGREDIENTS

Broccoli	2 medium sized	Light soya sauce	1 tblspn
Carrots	2 medium sized	Honey	1 tspn
Ginger	1 one inch knob	Refined oil	2 tblspns
Garlic cloves	4-6	Salt	to taste
Oranges	2 large sized	Pepper powder	to taste
Corn flour	2 tblspns		

METHOD OF PREPARATION

1. Wash the broccoli well and separate into small florets. Peel the stem and cut it into thin slices. Wash, peel and thinly slice the carrots.
2. Peel and thinly slice ginger and garlic.
3. Squeeze the juice of the orange and mix with the corn flour, soya sauce, honey and half cup of water. Reserve a little peel from the oranges. Gently scrape the fibrous membrane from the inner side of the orange peel, then cut into thin strips and keep them in cold water.
4. Heat oil in a pan, add broccoli stems and carrots and stir fry for about two minutes.
5. Add ginger, garlic and broccoli florets, stir-fry for another two minutes. Sprinkle a little water and cook for a few more minutes.
6. Stir in the orange juice mixture, cook on high heat for about a minute, stirring continuously. Do not overcook. Add salt and pepper.
7. Remove the orange rind strips from cold water and stir into the pan before serving.

NUTRITIONAL INFORMATION

Calories	180
Proteins	4.4
Fat	9
Carbohydrates	20.8
Fibre	2.3

Refined Oil:- Raw, unprocessed or crude oil usually needs a refining process to free it from undesirable taste, smell and colour. There are both desirable and undesirable effects of refining. For example palm crude oil when refined, loses a good amount of Betacarotene. On the other hand the taste, colour and flavour is much better with refined oil. Secondly, refined oil is a preferred medium for frying as it is devoid of impurities.

VEGETABLES IN THAI RED CURRY

INGREDIENTS

Carrots .... 4 medium sized

Capsicum .... 1 medium sized

Cauliflower .... ½ small sized

Cabbage .... ½ small sized

French beans .... 100 gms

Roasted peanuts .... 4 tblspns

Oil .... 1 tblspn

Lemon juice .... 1 tspn

Salt .... to taste

Thin coconut milk .... ¾ cup

Bean sprouts .... 100 gms

For Red Curry Paste

Dried whole red chillies 8

Lemon grass stalk .... 4 inches

Coriander seeds .... 4 tspns

Cumin seeds .... 2 tspns

Pepper corns 6

Onion, peeled and sliced ....

.... 2 medium sized

Garlic .... 4 cloves

Salt .... to taste

METHOD OF PREPARATION

1. Wash carrots and cut into three cm. long sticks.
2. Wash capsicum, halve, deseed and cut into three cm. long pieces.
3. Wash and cut cauliflower into small florets. Wash and cut cabbage into one centimetre sized pieces. Wash and string French beans and then cut them into three centimetre long pieces.
4. Crush roasted peanuts coarsely.
5. To make red curry paste, mix dried whole red chillies, lemon grass, coriander seeds, cumin seeds, pepper corns, chopped onion, garlic, salt and a little water, then grind into a fine paste.
6. Heat oil in a non-stick pan, add carrots, cauliflower, French beans and half a cup of water. Let it cook on medium heat for five to six minutes, stirring occasionally. Add cabbage and capsicum, mix well. Add red curry paste, stir well, cook on high heat for one or two minutes.
7. Stir in lemon juice and salt. Mix well and add thin coconut milk. Simmer for two minutes and stir in bean sprouts and crushed roasted peanuts.

SPROUTED MOONG CHAAT

INGREDIENTS

Potato .... 1 large sized

Sprouted green gram (*Moong*) ... 2 cups

Onions .... 2 medium sized

Tomatoes .... 2 medium sized

Cucumber .... 1 medium sized

Green chillies 4

Fresh coriander leaves .... a few sprigs

Chaat masala .... 1 tblspn

Lemon juice .... 2 tspns

Black salt .... to taste

METHOD OF PREPARATION

1. Boil the potato. Cool, peel and cut into one centimetre cubes.
2. Steam the sprouted *moong* in half a cup of water in a pressure cooker. Drain excess water and chill.
3. Peel and cut one onion into roundels, separate rings in each roundel and keep them in chilled water. Peel and chop the other onion.
4. Wash and finely chop tomatoes. Peel, deseed and cut the cucumbers into quarter inch sized. cubes.
5. Wash, remove stems, deseed and finely chop green chillies. Clean, wash and chop the coriander leaves.
6. In a bowl mix together potato, tomatoes, cucumber cubes, steamed sprouted *moong*, chopped onions and green chillies.
7. Just before serving, season with *chaat masala*, lemon juice and black salt. Mix well.
8. Serve chilled garnished with chopped coriander leaves and onion rings.

NUTRITIONAL INFORMATION

Calories	85
Proteins	3.9
Fat	0.3
Carbohydrates	17.1
Fibre	1.1

Chaat *is a typical Indian 'snacky' food item, mouthwatering temptation for many who find it hard to resist. Eating roadside chat is like feeding oneself with loads of calories. So a 'healthy' alternative is to choose 'sprouted* moong chaat', *which is not just low in calories but is an excellent source of many vitamins and minerals. Vitamin C, Beta-carotene, B complex are some of the important nutrients supplied by this dish.*

T I P *You may also top sprouted* moong chaat *with skimmed milk yogurt and tamarind chutney.*

ROSEMARY POTATOES

INGREDIENTS

Baby potatoes 16-20
Spring onions .... 2 medium sized
Cherry tomatoes 12-15
Fresh/dry rosemary .... 1 tspn

Olive oil .... 2 tblspns
Salt .... to taste
Paprika .... 1 tspn
Brown sugar .... 1 tspn

METHOD OF PREPARATION

1. Scrub and wash potatoes very well to remove any soil. Boil or roast them till they are three fourth done. Cool and halve.
2. Wash, trim and finely chop spring onions with the greens. Reserve chopped spring onion greens for garnish. Wash cherry tomatoes. If fresh rosemary is used wash and chop the rosemary.
3. Heat oil in a non-stick pan and add parboiled potato halves. Cook on high heat, tossing continuously till potatoes turn crisp and a little golden brown. Sprinkle chopped rosemary and spring onions. Mix well. Reduce heat and cook for another five minutes.
4. When the potatoes are fully done add cherry tomatoes to the pan. Season with salt, paprika and brown sugar.
5. Serve hot garnished with spring onion greens.

NUTRITIONAL INFORMATION

Calories	175
Proteins	1.7
Fat	8.3
Carbohydrates	25
Fibre	0.6

Rosemary, a common Caribbean herb, originates from the leaf part of the plant. It is not valued much for its food value. But as a stimulant to increase appetite and digestion, it holds an important place in the list of herbs.

MANGODI PANCHPHORAN

INGREDIENTS

Skimmed milk yogurt .... 1 cup
Bengal gram flour (*Besan*) .... 1 tblspn
Turmeric powder .... ½ tspn.
Red chilli powder .... 1½ tspns
Coriander powder .... 1 tblspn
Fresh coriander leaves .... ¼ cup
Green gram dumplings, dried (*Mangodi*)
.... 1 cup

Oil .... 1½ tspns
Mustard seeds .... ¼ tspn
Cumin seeds .... ½ tspn
Fennel seeds (*Saunf*) .... ½ tspn
Fenugreek seeds .... ¼ tspn
Asafoetida .... a pinch
Onion seeds (*Kalonji*) .... ¼ tspn
Salt .... to taste

METHOD OF PREPARATION

1. Whisk the yogurt with *besan*, turmeric powder, red chilli powder, coriander powder and one cup water. Ensure that there are no lumps. Clean, wash and chop the coriander leaves.
2. Heat a non-stick fry pan and dry roast the *mangodis*, stirring continuously till they turn golden brown. Remove and keep aside.
3. Heat oil in a pan. Add mustard seeds, cumin seeds, fennel seeds, fenugreek seeds, asafoetida and onion seeds. When they begin to crackle, reduce the heat and add the whisked yogurt mixture and salt to taste.
4. Stir well and bring it to a boil. Add roasted *mangodis* and chopped coriander leaves.
5. Reduce heat and simmer till the *mangodis* are soft and cooked. This requires approximately eight to ten minutes. However this time can change depending on the quality and size of *mangodis* that you use.

NUTRITIONAL INFORMATION

Calories	200
Proteins	11.8
Fat	4.3
Carbohydrates	27.2
Fibre	0.3

*Using **Mangodi** or **vadi** is an age old traditional method of adding variety and taste to various dishes and vegetables. It is a good source of protein and can be one of the good vegetarian substitutes for meat.*

T
I
P

Ready made sun-dried mangodis *are readily available at grocery stores.*

SICILIAN PASTA DON CAMILLO

INGREDIENTS

Eggplant .... 1 medium sized
Olive oil .... 1 tblspn
Tomatoes .... 2 medium sized
Garlic .... 4 cloves
Fresh basil .... a few leaves

Sun-dried tomatoes .... 50 gms
Spaghetti .... 200 gms
Salt .... to taste
Freshly crushed pepper ..... to taste

METHOD OF PREPARATION

1. Wash and cut the eggplant into half inch cubes. Brush them with olive oil and bake in preheated oven for fifteen minutes at 200 degrees Celsius.
2. Wash and cut tomatoes into small dices. Peel and chop garlic. Wash and tear basil leaves into small pieces. Reserve a few for garnish.
3. Clean and wash the sun-dried tomatoes and soak them in hot water for ten to fifteen minutes. Chop them roughly.
4. Boil sufficient water in a large pan and add spaghetti and cook till almost done. Strain and refresh in cold running water and keep it aside.
5. Heat olive oil in a pan, sauté chopped garlic and add diced tomatoes. Stir-fry for three to four minutes.
6. Add the baked eggplant cubes and stir-fry.
7. Add the cooked spaghetti, salt, freshly crushed pepper and basil leaves. Cook on medium heat for a couple of minutes, stirring continuously.
8. Just before serving, add the sun-dried tomatoes and toss. Serve hot garnished with the remaining basil leaves.

MIDDLE EASTERN VEGETABLE STEW

INGREDIENTS

Capsicum 1	Vegetable stock .... 3 cups
Zucchini .... 2 medium sized	Cloves 3-4
Celery .... 1 stem	Pepper corns 8-10
Carrots .... 2 medium sized	Cumin powder .... 1 tspn
Potatoes .... 2 medium sized	Red chilli powder .... a pinch
Chick peas .... ½ cup	Salt .... to taste
Ginger .... 1 one inch knob	Pepper powder .... ½ tspn
Mint leaves .... a few sprigs	

METHOD OF PREPARATION

1. Wash and cut the capsicum, zucchini and celery into two cm. sized pieces.
2. Wash, peel and cut the carrot into two cm. sized pieces. Wash, peel and dice the potatoes into two cm. sized pieces.
3. Wash and soak chick peas in sufficient water overnight. Pressure cook till they are done and keep them aside.
4. Peel and slice ginger. Clean, wash and chop the mint leaves.
5. Heat the vegetable stock in a saucepan and bring it to a boil.
6. Tie ginger slices, cloves and pepper corns in a muslin cloth and add it to the boiling stock.
7. Add the potatoes, boiled chick peas, carrots, celery, cumin powder and red chilli powder. Mix well and cook on medium heat till it begins to boil.
8. Cover and simmer on slow heat till all the vegetables are cooked and tender. Add the capsicum, and zucchini, cook for two minutes. Remove the bouquet of ginger, cloves and pepper corns.
9. Season with salt and pepper powder and garnish with chopped mint leaves. Serve hot.

NUTRITIONAL INFORMATION

Calories	95
Proteins	2.8
Fat	0.4
Carbohydrates	21.3
Fibre	1.5

Kabuli chana *is the popularly known name for chick peas. It is a good source of vegetarian protein, which accounts for about 25gms/100gms.*

It has a tough outer covering (indigestible fiber). It has low 'glycemic index' i.e. it takes long time to digest, absorb and therefore blood sugar levels rise very slowly after its consumption as against sugar where the blood sugar levels shoot up immediately. Including chickpeas in the diet of diabetics and weight watchers can be a great boon.

GARDEN FRESH EXOTICA

INGREDIENTS

Broccoli .... ½ medium sized
Snow peas (optional) 8-10
Button mushroom 6-8
Spring onions 2
Baby potatoes 3-4
French beans 5-6
Carrot .... 1 medium sized

Cauliflower .... ¼ medium sized
Fresh thyme .... few sprigs
Green peas, shelled .... ¼ cup
Olive oil .... 1 tblspn
Salt .... to taste
Pepper powder .... ½ tsp
Lemon juice .... 2 tspns

METHOD OF PREPARATION

1. Wash broccoli and cut into florets, string and cut snow peas into three pieces.
2. Wash and cut mushrooms into quarters, wash and slice spring onions diagonally.
3. Scrub and wash baby potatoes. Wash, string and cut French beans into diamond shape. Wash, peel and cut carrots into cubes.
4. Wash and cut cauliflower into florets. Wash and chop fresh thyme.
5. Boil the baby potatoes and keep aside.
6. Parboil (that is, cook them in boiling water till they are half cooked) broccoli, cauliflower, carrots, snow peas, french beans and green peas separately and keep aside.
7. In a pan heat some olive oil and sauté spring onions till they become translucent.
8. Add mushrooms and stir-fry for about two minutes, stirring continuously.
9. Add all parboiled vegetables and cook on high heat for a couple of minutes, tossing continuously.
10. Season it with salt and pepper powder. Add chopped thyme leaves.
11. Sprinkle lemon juice and serve hot.

PENNE WITH HERB & TOMATO SAUCE

INGREDIENTS

Tomatoes	8 medium sized	Bay leaf	1
Onions	1 medium sized	Water or vegetable stock	2 cups
Leek	1	Butter	1 tblspn
Celery	½ stem	Whole meal flour	2 tblspns
Capsicum	1	Skimmed milk	1 cup
Fresh basil	a few leaves	Salt	to taste
Penne pasta	200 gms	Pepper powder	1 tspn
Olive oil	1 tblspn	Mixed dry herbs	2 tspns

METHOD OF PREPARATION

1. Wash and roughly chop the tomatoes. Peel and chop onions. Wash the leek and celery and roughly chop them. Wash, deseed and dice capsicum into half inch sized pieces. Wash the basil leaves and keep them in cold water to be used for garnishing.
2. Boil penne pasta in plenty of water, do not overcook. Keep aside.
3. Heat olive oil in a pan and add bayleaf, chopped onions and sauté them till translucent. Add celery, leek and stir fry for a few minutes. Add the chopped tomatoes and sauté. Add water or stock and cook it on high heat for about ten minutes, stirring occasionally.
4. Reduce heat and simmer for about five minutes. Remove from heat and cool. Puree the tomato mixture in a blender.
5. Heat butter in a pan. Add whole meal flour and cook on medium heat for two to three minutes, stirring occasionally. Add skimmed milk, a little at a time, and stir continuously to avoid lumps.
6. Cook on low heat till you get the sauce consistency. Season with salt and pepper powder. Stir in pureed tomato sauce, diced capsicum and boiled penne pasta.
7. Heat the penne pasta thoroughly, add mixed dried herbs and serve hot garnished with basil leaves.

NUTRITIONAL INFORMATION

Calories	200
Proteins	2.3
Fat	3.9
Carbohydrates	11.4
Fibre	0.9

Leek has around 80% moisture and around 15 cals/100 gms. It has good amount of iron and Vitamin B1 (thiamin). Leek is the mildest of the onion family and a popular European vegetable. The white part of young leeks may be sliced thinly for salad or combined with other vegetables to flavour soups and stocks and cut in juliennes as a garnish.

T I P *Mixed dried herbs can be bought from the market or fresh herbs can be sun-dried and stored in an airtight container. Herbs that go well with this sauce are basil, thyme, chives and oregano.*

DAHI BHINDI

INGREDIENTS

Tender Ladyfingers (*Bhindi*) .... 400 gms
Green chillies 3-4
Ginger .... 1 one inch knob
Pepper corns .... ½ tspn
Skimmed milk yogurt .... 1½ cups
Bengal gram flour (*Besan*) . 1 tblspn

Oil .... 1½ tspns
Dry whole red chillies 2
Cumin seeds .... 1 tspn
Coriander powder .... 1 tblspn
Turmeric powder .... ½ tspn
Salt .... to taste

METHOD OF PREPARATION

1. Select tender and small ladyfingers. Wash and wipe them dry with a clean and absorbent kitchen towel.
2. Trim the stem and the tip. Wash green chillies, remove stem and then slit them.
3. Peel, wash and grind ginger with pepper corns to a fine paste.
4. Whisk skimmed milk yogurt.
5. Dry roast bengal gram flour (*besan*) in a non-stick pan on low heat, stirring continuously until it gives a roasted aroma. Keep aside to cool.
6. Heat oil in a non-stick pan, add dried whole red chillies, cumin seeds and stir-fry briefly.
7. Add green chillies, coriander powder, turmeric powder, *besan* and stir well.
8. Add trimmed ladyfingers, salt to taste and cook over medium heat, stirring frequently for five minutes.
9. Stir in the ginger and peppercorn paste. Reduce heat and add the whisked yogurt, mix well and cook covered for eight to ten minutes, stirring occasionally or until ladyfingers are completely cooked.

NUTRITIONAL INFORMATION

Calories	130
Proteins	4.9
Fat	6.1
Carbohydrates	12.3
Fibre	1.5

Bhindi *or ladyfinger has high moisture content (90%) and low fat (0.2%) which makes it a low-calorie vegetable. It is also a good source of fibre and has a fair amount of folic acid and zinc. Seeds of ladyfingers are a good source of protein.*

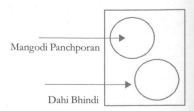

Mangodi Panchporan

Dahi Bhindi

PALAK BAHAR

INGREDIENTS

Spinach .... 2 bunches	Fresh coriander leaves ... a few sprigs
Green chillies 3	Oil .... 1½ tblspns
Carrots .... 2 medium sized	Nutmeg powder .... ¼ tspn
French beans 5-6	Cumin seeds .... ½ tspn
Cauliflower .... ¼ medium sized	Lemon juice .... 1 tspn
Onion............................ 1 large sized	Salt .... to taste
Tomatoes .... 2 medium sized	Red chilli powder .... 1 ½ tspns
Ginger .... 1 one inch knob	*Garam masala* powder .... 2 tspns
Garlic cloves 4	

METHOD OF PREPARATION

1. Wash a green chilli and remove its stem. Clean spinach under running water several times. Blanch it in boiling hot water for two to three minutes. Drain excess water and refresh spinach leaves in cold water. Puree it in a blender along with the green chilli.
2. Wash, peel and cut the carrots into thin diagonal slices. String the beans and cut into diamond shaped pieces. Wash and separate the cauliflower into small florets.
3. Peel and chop onion. Wash and chop the tomatoes. Peel and chop the ginger and garlic. Wash, remove stems and chop the remaining green chillies. Clean, wash and chop the coriander leaves.
4. Heat half the oil, add chopped ginger and garlic, stir fry.
5. Add chopped onion and green chillies, stir fry till onions are pinkish in colour. Add nutmeg powder and continue cooking on medium heat for a couple of minutes, stirring frequently.
6. Add pureed spinach, cook it for a minute and add salt. Keep it aside.
7. Blanch carrots, French beans and cauliflower.
8. Heat the remaining oil in a frying pan, add cumin seeds and when it starts to change colour, add chopped tomatoes. Cook on a medium heat for three to four minutes, stirring continuously. Add blanched vegetables and stir-fry lightly.
9. Add lemon juice and season with salt and red chilli powder. Lastly add *garam masala* powder and chopped coriander leaves.
10. Spread prepared spinach on a flat serving dish and place cooked vegetables in the centre and serve hot.

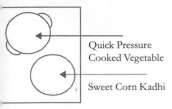

Quick Pressure
Cooked Vegetable

Sweet Corn Kadhi

ACCOMPANIMENTS

Accompaniments generally are not given their due importance though they are an essential part of a complete meal and play a very healthy role in our daily diet. They may be simple and minor in nature, but without them the main dish that they are supposed to accompany is incomplete. In other words they not only complement the main dish but also satisfy the senses of sight, smell and taste.

Apart from providing a variety, an accompaniment improves the nutritive value of the meal by contributing all the necessary nutrients that may be lacking in the main dish or the meal. The choice of an accompaniment is usually done with the intention of improving the overall suitability of the dish or the entire meal. For example, if the main dish is protein- rich, serve it with a dish that is high in fibre or starch. Similarly a spicy dish should ideally be served with a soothing dish.

Accompaniments can be broadly categorized into rice and breads. Though starch constitutes the bulk of the rice grain, it is the most easily and quickly digestible of all foods. Added to this, it has a considerable amount of proteins together with valuable B-complex vitamins and minerals like calcium, phosphorus and iron, which are very well utilized by the body. Wheat, on the other hand, has more proteins than rice. Its characteristic protein called gluten is what makes the bread dough stick together and gives it the ability to retain gas which is incorporated into the dough while kneading and without which the breads will turn out tough and heavy. Other than proteins, starch constitutes the bulk of the wheat grain together with calcium, phosphorus, iron and Vitamin B complex.

Many a times, due to its constituents, the accompaniment takes over the role of the main dish to provide a light meal and satisfy dietary requirement. When lentils, which are protein rich, and/or vegetables, which are vitamin and mineral rich, are added to either rice or wheat the resultant product can provide a complete meal in itself. Use of minimal or no oil will further enrich it by keeping the calories at the lowest level.

HERB AND ONION BREAD

INGREDIENTS

Fresh Yeast .... 20 gms
Sugar .... 1 tspn
Warm water .... 1 cup
Milk .... ½ cup
Butter .... 4 tblspns

Onion .... 2 medium sized
Whole wheat flour (*Atta*).. 2 ½ cups
Salt .... 1½ tspns
Mixed Herbs .... 1½ tspns

NUTRITIONAL INFORMATION

Calories	50
Proteins	1.6
Fat	1.2
Carbohydrates	8.5
Fibre	0.2

METHOD OF PREPARATION

1. Crumble yeast into a cup and sprinkle with the sugar. Add two tablespoons of warm water and mix until smooth.
2. Set in warm place for ten minutes, or until the mixture becomes frothy.
3. Pour the milk into a pan and heat gently. Remove from heat just before the milk begins to boil.
4. Chop the butter, drop into the milk and then add the remaining water.
5. Leave it for ten minutes or until the butter has completely melted and the milk becomes lukewarm.
6. Peel the onions and finely mince or grate them.
7. Put the flour and salt into a large basin. Add the herbs and the onion. Mix well.
8. Make a well in the centre and add the yeast mixture. With a light hand make a soft dough.
9. Cover with a damp cloth and leave it in a warm place for two hours, or until the dough has doubled in bulk.
10. Grease two bread tins of 450 grams each. Knead the dough well once again and divide into two portions.
11. Shape the dough into loaves and put them into the tins. Cover and leave for fermenting for forty five minutes or until the dough is almost double.
12. Bake in a preheated oven for forty five minutes at 180 degrees Celsius. Increase the heat to 220 degrees Celsius and bake for further twenty minutes.
13. Remove from the tins and cool on a wire tray. Slice and serve fresh and warm.

Whole wheat bread is more nutritious since it is made from the whole grain of wheat whereas white bread is made only from the starchy endosperm. Refined flour (maida) lacks the bran and germ and is low in vital nutrients. Hence products made from refined flour need to be enriched with added B complex and iron. Despite this addition, whole wheat bread contains significantly more fibre, vitamin B6, folic acid, magnesium and zinc than white bread. Whole grain products differ in two ways.

Whole grain bread and cereals are generally darker in colour and have a coarse texture. Also because they contain the germ, which contains oil, these turn rancid more quickly. While purchasing whole wheat bread, make sure the label states 100% Whole Wheat, which ascertains that it is truly whole grain bread. Very often, wheat breads are coloured with molasses to appear like whole wheat bread but are really white bread.

MIXED FLOUR METHI CHAPPATI

INGREDIENTS

Bengal gram flour (*Besan*) .... ½ cup
Whole meal flour (*Atta*) ...... ½ cup
Barley flour .... ½ cup
Salt .... to taste

Fenugreek leaves *(Methi)* .... 1 cup
Cabbage .... ¼ small sized
Skimmed milk yogurt .... ½ cup
Red chilli powder .... 1 tspr

METHOD OF PREPARATION

1. Sieve *besan*, wheat flour and barley flour along with salt.
2. Clean and wash *methi* in flowing water. Drain and finely chop the leaves. Finely grate cabbage.
3. Mix the chopped *methi* leaves and grated cabbage into the flour mixture. Add yogurt and red chilli powder. Add water, a little at a time, to make a medium soft dough. Knead well.
4. Keep it covered with a moist cloth for about fifteen minutes.
5. Divide the dough into eight to ten equal portions, and roll them into balls (*pedas*).
6. Heat a non-stick griddle plate (*tawa*) to medium heat. Roll out each portion of the dough into a disc of five to six inches diameter. Place it on the hot griddle plate and cook on one side for about half a minute.
7. Flip it over and cook the other side. Reduce heat and cook on both sides on low heat till light brown.
8. Serve hot.

PAUSHTIK BAJRE KI ROTI

INGREDIENTS

Millet (*Bajra*) flour .... 1 cup
Whole meal flour (*Atta*) ...... ¼ cup
Salt .... to taste
Onion .... 1 medium sized
Carrot .... 1 medium sized
Green chillies 2
Carom seeds (*Ajwain*) .... 1 tspn

METHOD OF PREPARATION

1. Sieve *bajra* flour, *atta* and salt together. Peel onion and grate. Wash carrot, peel and grate. Wash green chillies, remove stems and chop them finely.
2. Mix *bajra* flour, *atta* and salt mixture with grated onion, grated carrot, chopped green chillies and *ajwain*. Add water, a little at a time and knead the mixture into medium soft dough. Do not knead the dough excessively.
3. Divide the dough into eight equal portions and roll them into balls (*pedas*). Wet your palms, take a portion of dough and pat it between your palms to make a thin disc (*roti*) of about four to five inches diameter. Make it as thin as possible. It takes some practice before you can make thin *bajra* rotis.
4. Heat a non-stick griddle (*tawa*) and place the *roti* on it. First cook one side for about half a minute on medium heat and then flip it over and cook the other side similarly. Reduce flame and cook on slow heat on both sides till the *bajra roti* is slightly browned.
5. Repeat the same method with the remaining dough. Serve hot.

NUTRITIONAL INFORMATION

Calories	200
Proteins	6.3
Fat	2.2
Carbohydrates	39.3
Fibre	1.1

One of the important nutrients that bajra contains is **copper**. *Copper is involved in iron metabolism and nervous system functioning. It plays a role in the pigmentation of skin, hair and eyes. It is also required for cardiovascular and skeletal integrity.*

PALAK RAITA

INGREDIENTS

Spinach .... 2 medium sized bundles
Spring onions .... 2 medium sized
Garlic .... 3-4 cloves
Green chillies 2
Cumin seeds .... 2 tspns

Skimmed milk yogurt .... 2 cups
Black salt .... to taste
Red chilli powder .... 1 tspn
Oil .... ½ tspn
Salt .... ¼ tspn

METHOD OF PREPARATION

1. Clean, wash and chop spinach leaves. Clean, trim and chop spring onions with the greens. Peel and finely chop garlic. Wash, remove stems, deseed and finely chop green chillies.

2. Dry roast cumin seeds on a hot griddle plate (*tawa*) and grind to a fine powder.

3. Whisk the skimmed milk yogurt and add black salt, roasted cumin powder and red chilli powder. Mix well and chill in the refrigerator.

4. Heat oil in a non-stick pan, add chopped garlic and green chillies and stir-fry briefly. Add chopped spinach and spring onion along with its greens and sauté over high heat for three to four minutes, stirring continuously.

5. Season with salt and mix well. Continue to cook on high heat till the spinach is almost dry. Take it off the heat and cool. Mix with the seasoned yogurt just before serving.

SPINACH & CABBAGE PARANTHA

INGREDIENTS

Cabbage .... ¼ medium sized
Spinach .... 1 bunch
Green chillies............................. 2-3
Bengal gram flour (*Besan*) .... ½ cup
Whole meal flour .... 2 cups
Salt...to taste

Carom seeds (*Ajwain*) .... ½ tspn
Red chilli powder .... 1 tspn
Asafoetida .... a pinch
Skimmed milk .... ½ cup
Oil .... 8 tspns

METHOD OF PREPARATION

1. Wash and grate the cabbage after removing the middle stem.
2. Wash the spinach under running water several times, break stem from each leaf and then finely chop. Wash, remove stems, deseed and chop green chillies.
3. Sieve *besan* and whole meal flour along with salt. Add *ajwain*, red chilli powder and asafoetida..
4. Add chopped spinach, grated cabbage, chopped green chillies and skimmed milk. Make a medium soft dough.
5. Cover the dough with a damp muslin cloth and keep aside for fifteen minutes.
6. Divide the dough into eight equal portions and shape them into balls.
7. Using a little flour, roll out each ball into diskettes of five to six inches diameter.
8. Heat a non-stick griddle (*tawa*) on medium heat. Place the rolled out parantha on the hot griddle and cook on one side for half a minute.
9. Flip it over and cook the other side. Apply very little oil to the first cooked side, increase heat and cook the oiled side pressing it all round with a flat spoon; turn the side and sprinkle a little oil on this side also.
10. Cook on medium to low heat for a minute, turning it once more.
11. Serve hot with pickle and *raita* of your choice.

NUTRITIONAL INFORMATION

Calories	165
Proteins	5
Fat	5.8
Carbohydrates	22.3
Fibre	0.7

Ajwain, also known as Omum is an important medicinal spice in our kitchen. It is known to be an effective remedy for colds and sore throat. Its distinct aroma and a pungent taste gives it an important place in Indian cookery.

Apart from this it is very high in calcium, phosphorus, iron, manganese, copper and other trace minerals.

T I P *If you make this parantha without any oil, the total calorie content per parantha would reduce to 120 and fat to 0.8 gms.*

THREE AROMA VEGETABLE RICE

INGREDIENTS

Rice .... 1 ½ cups
Salt .... to taste
Carrots .... 2 medium sized
Lemon grass .... 2 inch stalk
Cauliflower .... ¼ small sized
Cabbage .... ¼ small sized
Spinach 12-16

Corn flour .... 1 ½ tblspns
Star anise 2
Shelled green peas .... ½ cup
Crushed black pepper .... 1 tblspn
Soya sauce .... 1 tblspn
Sesame oil .... 1 tspn

NUTRITIONAL INFORMATION

Calories	220
Proteins	5.7
Fat	1.5
Carbohydrates	48.3
Fibre	1.3

*A lot of vegetables are used in this recipe. **Trimming** is essential for removal of decayed or inedible parts. Often parts of foods are discarded for reason of palatability, even if the part is edible. Certain kind of trimming of fruits and vegetables can significantly reduce the micronutrient, which tends to be more concentrated in a thin layer right under the skin rather than in the inner parts of many fruits and vegetables. Also the dark outer leaves of vegetables such as lettuce, broccoli and celery are higher in micronutrients than are other parts of the vegetables.*

METHOD OF PREPARATION

1. Pick and wash rice in plenty of water and then soak for about half an hour. Drain well.
2. Boil rice in salted boiling water until completely cooked. Drain and keep warm.
3. Wash, peel and cut carrots into half centimetre cubes. Wash lemon grass stalk.
4. Separate cauliflower into small florets and wash them. Soak them in warm salted water and keep aside.
5. Cut cabbage into half centimetre chunks. Clean, wash and trim spinach leaves.
6. Dissolve corn flour in half cup water.
7. Take three cups of water in a pan, add lemon grass, star anise and carrots and bring it to a boil. Continue to cook in boiling water for three minutes, reduce heat and add green peas and cauliflower florets.
8. Simmer till green peas and carrots are just done. Stir in cabbage and spinach leaves. Season with salt and crushed pepper corn.
9. Add soya sauce, bring it to a boil and stir in corn flour dissolved in water while stirring continuously. Simmer for half a minute. Arrange rice in a large service bowl and pour cooked vegetables over the rice and sprinkle sesame oil on top.
10. Serve immediately.

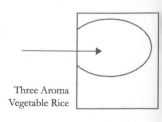

Three Aroma
Vegetable Rice

MUSHROOM DUM BIRYANI

INGREDIENTS

Fresh button mushrooms .... 15-20 medium sized.	Green cardamoms 2
Basmati rice ....1½ cups	Black cardamoms 2
Onions .... 2 medium sized	Cinnamon .... 1 inch piece
Ginger .... 1 one inch knob	Mace .... 1 blade
Garlic .... 5 cloves	Salt .... to taste
Green coriander leaves .... ¼ cup	Oil ....2 tspns
Fresh mint leaves .... ¼ cup	Red chilli powder ....2 tspns
Tomatoes .... 2 medium sized	Coriander powder .... 1 tblspn
Skimmed milk yogurt .... ½ cup	Crushed peppercorn .... ½ tblspn
Saffron .... a generous pinch	Cumin powder ....½ tspn
Skimmed milk .... ¼ cup	Turmeric powder ....½ tspn
Bay leaf 1	*Garam masala* powder ....½ tspn
Cloves 4	*Kewra* water (optional) .... 4-5 drops

METHOD OF PREPARATION

1. Scrub and wash mushrooms, drain and cut into quarters.
2. Pick and wash basmati rice in plenty of water and soak in sufficient water for half an hour.
3. Peel and finely slice onions. Peel ginger, garlic and grind together to a fine paste. Clean, wash and finely chop fresh coriander and mint leaves.
4. Wash tomatoes and make a puree in a blender. Whisk the skimmed milk yogurt and keep. Soak the saffron in one fourth cup warm skimmed milk.
5. Boil three to four cups water in a thick bottomed vessel, add bay leaf, cloves, green cardamoms, black cardamoms, cinnamon, mace and one teaspoon salt. When the water starts boiling rapidly, drain the soaked basmati rice and add.
6. Cook for eight to ten minutes, stirring frequently or until the rice is three fourth done. Drain in a colander.

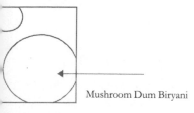

Mushroom Dum Biryani

7. Heat oil in a non stick pan, add sliced onions and stir-fry over high heat for two to three minutes or until the onion turns translucent. Add ginger-garlic paste and cook briefly.

8. Add red chilli powder, coriander powder, crushed peppercorn, cumin powder and turmeric powder. Stir-fry briefly and add the pureed tomatoes.

9. Continue cooking over high heat for another two to three minutes, stirring continuously or until *masala* is fairly thick.

10. Add the whisked skimmed milk yogurt, *garam masala* powder and half the quantity of chopped fresh coriander and mint leaves. Stir well and cook for two minutes more.

11. Add the quartered button mushrooms and salt to taste. Stir-fry over high heat for two to three minutes and remove from heat.

12. Arrange the cooked rice and mushroom *masala* in alternate layers in an oven proof dish (or Biryani *handi*), sprinkle the chopped fresh coriander and mint leaves, *kewra* water and the skimmed milk with saffron. Ensure that the top most layer is of rice.

13. Cover the assembled biryani with a tight fitting lid and seal the edges with kneaded *atta* dough (if required).

14. Keep the sealed dish on a medium hot *tawa* and leave for ten to fifteen minutes. You can also place a few burning charcoals on the lid. Alternately, leave the sealed dish in a pre-heated oven for ten to fifteen minutes.

15. Break the seal and open the biryani, just before serving.

NUTRITIONAL INFORMATION

Calories	205
Proteins	5.3
Fat	4.2
Carbohydrates	36.3
Fibre	0.4

Cloves are aromatic and are effective stimulants for the lungs and stomach. They work against cold and are good disinfectants for teeth. Cloves are rich in iron and manganese. Manganese though required in small amount, has important functions to perform in the body. It is a component of many enzymes. Its deficiency can lead to abnormality in skeletal bone mineralisation.

TASTY PROTEIN PULAO

INGREDIENTS

Basmati rice .... 1 ¼ cups	Oil .... 1 ½ tspns
Onion...................... 1 medium sized	Coriander powder .... 2 tspns
Ginger .... 1 one inch knob	Turmeric powder .... 1 tspn
Tomatoes .... 2 medium sized	Red chilli powder .... 1 tspn
Fresh coriander leaves.......... ¼ cup	*Garam masala* powder .... 1 tspn
Soya chunks .... 1 ½ cups	Salt .... to taste
Cumin seeds .... 1 tspn	

METHOD OF PREPARATION

1. Pick and wash basmati rice in plenty of water and soak in sufficient water for half an hour.
2. Peel and chop onion and ginger. Wash and chop tomatoes. Clean, wash and finely chop fresh coriander leaves.
3. Soak soya chunks in lukewarm water for fifteen minutes. Squeeze to remove excess water and cut each piece into two.
4. Heat oil in a thick-bottomed pan, add cumin seeds and let them crackle. Add chopped onions and sauté for two minutes. Cook on medium heat, stirring continuously till onions turn brown.
5. Add coriander powder, turmeric powder, red chilli powder and chopped tomatoes. Continue cooking on medium heat for three to four minutes or until tomatoes are cooked.
6. Add soya chunks, basmati rice and chopped fresh coriander leaves and stir gently for a minute. Stir in three cups of water, *garam masala* powder, salt to taste and bring it to a boil.
7. Reduce the heat, cover the pan and simmer till all the water has been absorbed and rice is cooked. Serve hot.

NUTRITIONAL INFORMATION

Calories	195
Proteins	10.4
Fat	2
Carbohydrates	27.9
Fibre	0.4

Soya flour can be processed and extruded to give textured chunks, called protein isolates or meat alternatives. These chunks when soaked and cooked appear remarkably like meat. Such products are not only less costly than meat but score more even on health ground. They have no cholesterol, no saturated fat. Soya chunks are a good source of protein which is high in both quality and quantity.

SPROUTED MOONG KHICHDI

INGREDIENTS

Rice .... 1 cup	Cinnamon .... 1 inch stick
Carrots .... 2 medium sized	Turmeric powder .... ½ tspn
Cauliflower .... ½ medium sized	Crushed Pepper corns .... ½ tblspn
Green chillies 3-4	Salt .... to taste
Pure *Ghee* .... 1 tspn	Sprouted green gram (whole *Moong*)
Cumin seeds .... 1 tspn	.... 1 ½ cups

NUTRITIONAL INFORMATION

Calories	180
Proteins	6.5
Fat	1.5
Carbohydrates	35.6
Fibre	1.3

Ghee *is highly valued in ancient medicine as a rejuvenative food. According to Ayurveda,* ghee *is cool, light and oily.* Ghee *aids the digestion and absorption of other nutrients. Homemade* ghee *is valued more for its taste, aroma and medicinal properties. However, ghee, either homemade or purchased from the market, gives 9 calories/ gm or 45 calories/ tspn.*

METHOD OF PREPARATION

1. Pick and wash rice in plenty of water and soak in sufficient water for half hour. Wash, peel and cut carrots into one inch sized pieces.
2. Wash and cut cauliflower into small florets. Wash green chillies, remo stems and slit them into two.
3. Heat ghee in a non-stick pan and add cumin seeds. Stir-fry over high heat they start changing colour.
4. Add cinnamon stick, turmeric powder, crushed pepper corns and slit gre chillies; stir-fry for a while. Add the cut carrots and cauliflower and mix w
5. Drain and add the soaked rice and salt to taste, stir briefly and add two a half cups of water.
6. Bring the rice to a rapid boil, add the sprouted *moong*, reduce heat and simn for fifteen to twenty minutes, stirring frequently or until the rice is ligh mashed and completely cooked.

T I P *Though ghee has high saturated fat, we have used very low quantity here.*

VEGETABLE FRIED RICE WITH HERBS

INGREDIENTS

Rice .... 1 cup	Groundnut oil .... 1½ tspns
Capsicums .... 2 medium sized	Five spice powder .... 1½ tspns
French beans 10	Dried mixed herbs .... 1 tspn
Baby corns 4	Shelled green peas .... ¼ cup
Bamboo shoots in brine .... 2-3 slices	Light soya sauce .... 2 tspns
Garlic .... 4 cloves	Salt .... to taste
Fresh coriander leaves ... a few sprigs	Pepper powder .... to taste
Mint leaves .... a few sprigs	White vinegar .... 2 tspns

METHOD OF PREPARATION

1. Wash and soak rice in sufficient water for at least half an hour. Cook it in plenty of salted boiling water till almost done. Drain and keep aside.
2. Wash, deseed and cut capsicum into one centimetre cubes. String, wash and cut French beans diagonally into diamonds. Boil green peas in boiling hot water till done, drain and refresh in cold water. In case you are using frozen green peas, do not boil.
3. Wash and diagonally cut baby corns into one centimetre slices. Wash and cut bamboo shoot into 1 cm. cubes.
4. Peel the garlic cloves, wash and crush them. Clean, wash and finely chop coriander and mint leaves.
5. Heat oil in a non-stick wok or a frying pan, add crushed garlic and stir-fry on high heat.
6. Add capsicum, baby corns, French beans, peas, bamboo shoot and soya sauce, keep stirring all the time. Sprinkle five spice powder and dried mixed herbs. Cook for about half a minute on high heat, stirring continuously.
7. Add the rice, stir-fry briefly, add chopped coriander and mint. Season it with salt and pepper powder. Add vinegar and mix well.
8. Serve hot.

NUTRITIONAL INFORMATION

Calories	150
Proteins	3.7
Fat	2.5
Carbohydrates	27.9
Fibre	1

Tender bamboo shoots are low in calorie (40 cals/ 100 gms). They have good amount of B2 (Riboflavin) vitamin. To prepare them, remove the tough outer skin and boil them in water for some time. Adding some bell pepper to the water helps to remove the bitter taste.

JADE FRIED RICE

INGREDIENTS

Rice	1 cup	Vegetable oil	1 tspn
Zucchini	1 medium sized	Soya sauce	2 tspns
Carrot	1 medium sized	Brown sugar	2 tspns
Spinach	1 bunch	Salt	to taste
Garlic	4 cloves	Pepper powder	½ tspn
Ginger	½ inch knob		

NUTRITIONAL INFORMATION

Calories	135
Proteins	2.9
Fat	1.4
Carbohydrates	27.2
Fibre	0.7

The way rice is cooked affects its nutritional quality. The water is almost totally absorbed when rice is cooked in a pressure cooker or a rice cooker.

However, when rice is cooked in an open pan and the excess water discarded, the water contains not just starch but also some water-soluble mineral and vitamins.

METHOD OF PREPARATION

1. Wash and cut zucchini into one centimetre sized cubes. Wash, peel and cut carrot into matchstick size pieces. Clean spinach, wash thoroughly and break into small pieces by hand or roughly chop. Wash, peel and finely chop the garlic and ginger.
2. Clean, wash and soak rice for about half an hour. Cook the rice in sufficient boiling water, drain and rinse under cold running water.
3. Heat oil in a pan or wok, add chopped garlic and ginger and stir-fry for half a minute.
4. Add the carrot pieces, cubed zucchini and stir-fry for further two minutes taking care that the vegetables still retain their crunchiness.
5. Add the spinach, soya sauce, brown sugar and rice.
6. Mix well and season with salt and pepper powder. Serve hot.

TOMATO & BLACK MUSHROOM RISOTTO

INGREDIENTS

Rice, preferably Arborio ... 1½ cups
Tomatoes .... 3 medium sized
Black mushrooms 10-12
Butter .... 1 tblspn
White wine .... ¼ cup
Vegetable stock .... 2 cups

Skimmed milk .... 1 cup
Salt .... to taste
Pepper powder .... ½ tspn
Low fat cheese .... ¼ cup
Cherry tomatoes 8-10

METHOD OF PREPARATION

1. Wash the rice. For making risotto there is no need to soak the rice.
2. Blanch the tomatoes by putting them in boiling water for ten seconds and immediately transferring them to a bowl of cold water. Remove skin and deseed them. Chop them finely.
3. Soak the mushrooms in hot water, drain and roughly chop them.
4. In a thick-bottomed pan, heat half of the butter on medium heat and add the chopped tomatoes. Sauté them till they are cooked.
5. Add the chopped mushrooms and stir-fry. Add the Arborio rice and sauté for three to four minutes; add white wine and cook on high heat for a couple of minutes, stirring frequently.
6. Stir in stock followed by half the quantity of skimmed milk. Reduce heat and cook on medium heat, stirring gently and continuously.
7. Cook the rice till it is done, stirring all the time. Season with salt and pepper.
8. Just before serving, add the grated cheese and remaining butter and skimmed milk to give it a creamy texture. Top it with cherry tomatoes and serve hot.

NUTRITIONAL INFORMATION

Calories	245
Proteins	8.3
Fat	6.6
Carbohydrates	36.8
Fibre	0.6

Skimmed milk in simple language is milk from which fat is skimmed off (removed). This milk has 0.1% fat as compared to 6.5% in buffalo's milk and 4% in cow's milk, 3% in toned milk. Please note that protein is also skimmed off along with fat and so is Vitamin A (as Vitamin A is fat soluble) and weight watchers need to make up for these nutrients from other food sources.

T
I
P
The consistency of a risotto is quite thick and lumpy, therefore the rice that you choose should be thick and starchy. If you cannot get Arborio rice or find it too expensive, use rice that you would normally use for making khichdi.

PITA BREAD

INGREDIENTS

Refined flour .... 1 cup

Whole meal wheat flour .... 1 cup

Dried yeast .... 1 tblspn

Or fresh yeast .... 1 tspn

Salt .... 1 tspn

Sugar .... 1 tspn

Water .... 1 $\frac{1}{3}$ cups

METHOD OF PREPARATION

1. Preheat the oven at 230 degrees Celsius.
2. Sieve the refined flour, whole meal flour and salt together.
3. In a small bowl take yeast and sugar, pour four tablespoons lukewarm water over it, sprinkle a little flour, cover and keep aside.
4. Keep some flour aside for dusting and take the rest of the flour in a bowl making a well in the centre of the flour. Pour in the yeast mixture and mix in a little flour from the sides of the well. Make a soft dough using the remaining water and kneading really well.
5. Keep the dough aside for one hour to rise.
6. Knead the dough again very lightly and divide it into eight equal portions. Shape them into balls and leave aside for ten to fifteen minutes, covered with a damp cloth. Roll out the pieces into ovals (five by eight inches) and again keep them aside for twenty minutes, covered with a damp cloth.
7. Grease and flour baking sheets. Place them in the oven for five minutes. Arrange the Pita breads on them and put in the oven for fifteen minutes. In this time they will start turning brown.
8. Cool them on wire racks and store.

DESSERTS

Desserts form an important part of any meal but more importantly of a festive one. Be it in India or in any other place in the world, a sweet dish generally rounds off a sumptuous meal.

The repertoire of Indian sweets is an impressive one though the Western desserts do not lag far behind. However, there are differences between the traditional Indian sweets and their Western counterparts. The most distinct one being that Indian sweets can be or are served along with the meal whereas Western desserts are served after the meal.

The basic ingredients of most Western desserts, unlike Indian sweets, are refined flour, fat (margarine, butter, cream), eggs and sugar thus rendering the products rich in calories and fat. The egg yolks add to the cholesterol levels besides making them rich in proteins.

These desserts can be made more health oriented by using substitute ingredients like whole meal flour (instead of refined one), fresh fruits (poached, broiled or made into compote) instead of sugar, skimmed milk, skimmed milk yogurt and low fat cream instead of whole milk, whole cream. This way not only are the calories reduced but the desserts become rich in fibre, vitamins and minerals.

Similarly the Indian sweets too can be made within the desirable calorie limits without affecting their taste by using similar ingredients. Using substitute cooking methods — steaming and baking instead of frying — the low calorie values can be maintained. Quality sugar substitutes are now available in the market and are safe to use and do not take away the taste value from the desserts to which they are added.

The desserts that are given here are both low in calories and tasty and can be safely consumed by the young and old, by diabetics or the weight conscious or even by heart patients.

ORANGE RICE PUDDING

INGREDIENTS

Rice	¹/₃ cup	Skimmed milk	2 cups
Raisins	½ cup	Honey	1½ tblspns
Seedless dates	6-8	Vanilla essence	¼ tspn
Orange rind	1 tspn	Fresh orange juice	½ cup

METHOD OF PREPARATION

1. Pick, wash and soak rice in sufficient water for half an hour. Soak raisins in water for fifteen minutes. Squeeze out excess water. Chop dates roughly. Finely shred orange rind.
2. Boil milk in a non-stick saucepan. Drain and add rice to the boiling milk, reduce heat and cook, stirring continuously till the rice is soft and the milk is completely absorbed.
3. Remove from heat and cool to room temperature. Combine cooked rice with honey, raisins, vanilla essence, chopped dates, shredded orange rind and fresh orange juice.
4. Pour into a medium sized ceramic or glass ovenproof dish. Bake the pudding in the preheated oven at 160 degrees Celsius for fifteen minutes.
5. Serve warm or chilled.

STRAWBERRY CHEESE CAKE

INGREDIENTS

Crust
Bran biscuit or Digestive biscuit ... 8-10
Margarine .... 1 tblspn
Instant coffee powder .... 1 tspn
Filling
Fresh Strawberry ... 12 medium sized
Skimmed milk yogurt .... 1½ cups
Skimmed milk cottage cheese ....
.... 1½ cups
Powdered sugar .... ½ cup

Carrageenan .... 15 gms
Skimmed milk .... 1 cup
Corn flour .... 1 tblspn
Lemon rind .... of one lemon
Vanilla essence .... 1 tspn
Strawberry essence .... 1 tspn
Topping
Fresh Strawberry ..... 6-8 medium sized
Strawberry or lemon jelly .... 1 tblspn

METHOD OF PREPARATION

1. Crush biscuits to coarse powder. Melt margarine. Dissolve instant coffee powder in two teaspoons boiling water, cool slightly. Combine melted margarine and dissolved coffee with the crushed biscuits.
2. Line a six inch spring form pan with butter paper. Press mixture evenly over bottom of the prepared pan. Set aside.
3. Soak the carregnan in quarter cup water. Heat it lightly on a double boiler to dissolve and keep warm. Hull strawberries and roughly chop.
4. Dissolve the cornflour in two tablespoons of milk and add it to the rest of milk. Cook it on low heat till it thickens. Take it off the heat and cool it to the room temperature.
5. Hang yogurt in a muslin cloth for about half an hour. Place cottage cheese and hung yogurt in food processor or blender. Process until smooth. Add the other filling ingredients. Process just until blended, scraping sides of bowl frequently.
6. Pour filling into the prepared pan. Cover and chill until set, for at least two hours.
7. Meanwhile hull and slice strawberries. Dissolve strawberry or lemon jelly in quarter cup water, bring it to a boil and cool.
8. Decorate the top of the chilled cheesecake with sliced strawberries and brush liberally with the prepared jelly. Chill until the jelly is set.
9. Remove from the spring form pan and cut into eight wedges with a sharp knife dipped in hot water.

T I P *Spring form pan is similar to a round shallow cake tin but with a removable base. Carregnan is a vegetable alternative to geletin.*

GUR AUR BADAM KI PHIRNI

INGREDIENTS

Pistachio nuts 4-6	Jaggery (*Gur*) .... 4 tblspns
Cashew nuts 6-8	Cardamom powder .... ½ tspn
Rice .... ¼ cup	Rose water .... 1 tspn
Skimmed milk .... 3 cups	

METHOD OF PREPARATION

1. Soak pistachio nuts and almonds in hot water for five minutes. Drain, peel and cut pistachio nuts into slivers. Crush almonds into small bits.
2. Pick, wash and soak rice in sufficient water for thirty minutes. Drain and grind the soaked rice into fairly smooth paste. Dilute the rice paste in half cup of water and keep aside.
3. Boil milk in a non-stick saucepan, reduce heat, and add ground rice mixture. Cook on medium heat for about five minutes, stirring continuously or till the mixture thickens.
4. Add jaggery, crushed cashew nuts and cardamom powder. Reduce heat and cook till jaggery has completely dissolved. (You may notice a little curdling of milk, ignore as it is quite common for some varieties of jaggery to have this effect on milk.)
5. Remove from heat, stir in rose water and pour into separate serving bowls, preferably earthenware. Garnish with slivered pistachio nuts.
6. Chill it in refrigerator for an hour before serving.

NUTRITIONAL INFORMATION

Calories	156
Proteins	7.2
Fat	5.0
Carbohydrates	9.0
Fibre	0.3

Almond is a rich source of calories, proteins, zinc and manganese. It is also an excellent source of Vitamin E, second only to wheat germ. Vitamin E helps protect cells from free radical injury. Hence it serves as an anti-oxidant and may help protect against heart disease, cataracts and certain cancers. It is needed for normal growth and development.

KESARI PHIRNI

INGREDIENTS

Skimmed milk .... 2 ½ cups	Saffron .... a few strands
Pistachio nuts 6-8	Sugar substitute (Equal Spoonful,
Cardamom powder .... ½ tspn	etc.) .... 4 tblspns
Rice flour, coarse .... 6 tblspns	

METHOD OF PREPARATION

1. Boil milk and keep aside.
2. Blanch pistachio nuts in hot water, remove skin and slice finely.
3. Mix the rice flour in half cup water and make a fine paste without any lumps.
4. Add this paste to the milk and bring it to a boil.
5. When it starts to thicken, reduce heat and simmer for a couple of minutes, stirring continuously. Add cardamom powder and saffron and mix well.
6. When it becomes thick and reaches custard like consistency, remove from heat and stir in sugar substitute.
7. Pour the mixture into four individual earthenware bowls while it is still warm. Sprinkle sliced pistachio nuts and refrigerate for at least two hours.
8. Serve chilled.

NUTRITIONAL INFORMATION

Calories	80
Proteins	4.2
Fat	1.3
Carbohydrates	14.7
Fibre	0.1

Sugar substitutes_ or artificial sweeteners provide the same sweetness as sugar does without the added calories. It is a boon to diabetics and calorie conscious people who can have sweets and desserts without fear.

Aspartame, used to sweeten a variety of foods and beverages, is one of the most thoroughly tested food ingredients ever used. Its use is generally considered safe.

However, people who have the rare disease — phenylketonuria (PKU) should not eat or drink anything containing aspartame.

T I P *Sweet dishes with empty calories are a definite no-no for the calorie conscious. Therefore we have suggested a sugar substitute like Equal Spoonful. However it may be prudent to check with your doctor if you have any special health condition which restricts your use of sugar substitutes.*

APPLE CAKE

INGREDIENTS

Whole meal flour (*Atta*) .... 1 cup
Refined flour (*Maida*) .... 1 cup
Baking powder .... 2 tspns.
Soda-bi-carbonate .... ½ tspn.
Cinnamon powder............. ¼ tspn.

Powdered Sugar .... 1 cup
Butter (melted) .... 150 gms.
Apple puree (unsweetened)1½ cups
Skimmed milk .... 1 cup

METHOD OF PREPARATION

1. Take a cake tin of one kilogram capacity, grease it with oil/fat, sprinkle with a little flour and dust off the excess. Keep it aside.
2. Preheat the oven to 200 degrees Celsius.
3. Sieve the flour, baking powder, soda-bi-carbonate, cinnamon powder and powdered sugar together.
4. Mix together skimmed milk and unsweetened apple puree till well blended. Add the melted butter and mix again.
5. Gradually add the flour mixture, stirring well to prevent the formation of lumps.
6. If the mixture is too thick add a little water or skimmed milk to get the right consistency.
7. Put the mixture in the well-greased cake tin and bake in the preheated oven at 200 degrees Celsius for thirty to forty minutes.
8. Allow the cake to cool down properly before cutting it.

POACHED CINNAMON APPLE

INGREDIENTS

Apples .... 4 medium sized
Dried figs 2-3
Brown sugar .... 2 tblspns
Raisins .... 3-4 tblspns
Lemon juice .... 1 tspn
Cinnamon powder .... 1 tspn
Red wine .... ½ cup
Unsweetened apple juice .... 1 cup

METHOD OF PREPARATION

1. Wash, core and pat dry apples. Prick them with a fork. Chop the dry figs.
2. Make a filling using brown sugar, raisins, chopped dry figs, lemon juice and cinnamon powder.
3. Stuff the apples with this raisins and figs filling.
4. Arrange the apples on a baking dish or ovenproof dish and pour the wine and apple juice.
5. Bake in a preheated oven at 175 degrees Celsius for thirty to forty minutes.
6. When slightly cooled, halve the apples.
7. Serve warm. It can also be served at room temperature or chilled.

NUTRITIONAL INFORMATION

Calories	105
Proteins	0.2
Fat	0.3
Carbohydrates	24.9
Fibre	0.6

*One **dry fig** weighs about 20 gms and will give 60 cals, 1 gm protein and 0gm fat. Figs are rich source of thiamin, iron and calcium. Figs are known to have laxative property and are often advised for constipation. It is one of the wholesome natural foods that can be enjoyed by all.*

PEAR PARADISE

INGREDIENTS

Pears .... 4 large sized
Lemon juice .... 1 tblspn
Orange rind .... 1 tblspn
Pistachio nuts 6-8

Unsweetened mango pulp ... ½ cup
Fresh orange juice .... 1 cup
Sherry (optional) .... 4 tblspns

METHOD OF PREPARATION

NUTRITIONAL INFORMATION

Calories	100
Proteins	1.5
Fat	2
Carbohydrates	18.2
Fibre	1.3

*It should be noted that in this dish **Pistachio** nuts are used only for garnishing, which do not affect its caloric content to any great extent. Pistachios are high in fat (53%) and calories (650/100 gms.). People on a low calorie diet or those suffering from heart diseases, should avoid eating nuts and dry fruits. However if this dish is prepared for kids, then the amount of pistachios can be increased since they also have a good amount of other micro-nutrients, protein (20%) calcium, phosphorous and iron.*

1. Wash, peel and halve pears. Remove seeds, apply lemon juice and keep aside.
2. Cut orange rind into thin strips. Soak the pistachios in hot water for five minutes. Drain, peel and slice.
3. Arrange pears with the cut side facing down in a medium sized oven-proof ceramic or glass dish. Mix unsweetened mango pulp, orange rind, fresh orange juice, sherry and pour on the arranged pears.
4. Bake in a preheated oven at 180 degrees Celsius for thirty minutes. Alternatively cook in a microwave oven on HIGH mode for five minutes.
5. Garnish with sliced pistachios and serve warm. You may also serve this chilled, if desired.

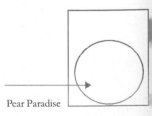

Pear Paradise

T I P *You can use the pear peel in your regular chutney and make it more tasty and nutritious.*

MEDLEY OF FRUITS WITH CANDIED ROSE

INGREDIENTS

Watermelon .... 1/4 medium sized
Pineapple .... 1/4 medium sized
Apples .... 2 medium sized
Lemon juice .... 1 tspn
Pomegranate ...... 1/2 medium sized
Bananas 1

Orange 1
Sweet lime 1
Chickoo 1
Candied rose petals(*Gulkand*) ....
.... 2 tblspns
Fresh orange or sweetlime juice . 1 cup

METHOD OF PREPARATION

1. Scoop out watermelon into small balls, using a Parisienne scoop. Scoop out pineapple also into small balls.
2. Scoop apples into small sized balls and sprinkle with lemon juice and mix well.
3. Peel pomegranate and separate the pomegranate pearls. Peel and slice the banana into six to eight pieces.
4. Peel orange, deseed, remove the white pith and cut the segments into two.
5. Peel sweet lime, deseed, remove the white pith and cut the segments into two. Peel, remove seeds and cut chikoo into thin wedges.
6. Mix candied rose petals (*gulkand*) with fresh orange juice or fresh sweet lime juice.
7. Arrange the fruits in a serving plate decoratively and refrigerate.
8. Just before serving lace candied rose petal and fresh juice mixture on to the arranged fruits. Serve immediately.

NUTRITIONAL INFORMATION

Calories	175
Proteins	1. 5
Fat	8
Carbohydrates	39. 6
Fibre	2. 1

Pomegranate, *like other fruits is an excellent source of minerals and micronutrients. This dish is rich in all minerals like phosphorous, potassium, manganese and magnesium, to name a few. Magnesium activates about 100 enzymes in our body and helps nerve and muscle functions. It has been discovered that pomegranate contains a unique fatty acid called punicic acid, believed to give the fruit its healing powers to combat ageing. Researchers also discovered that pomegranate has chemicals that fight heart diseases and cancer.*

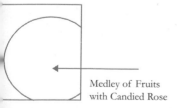

Medley of Fruits
with Candied Rose

T
I *Instead of making scoops out of fruits, you can also prepare this dessert by cutting the fruits*
P *into any shape.*

FROM THE NUTRITIONIST'S DESK
Selecting Your Diet

Our effort here is to give you these wholesome low calorie recipes which can become a part of your everyday meal. Indeed for many of us the meaning of 'dieting' is to avoid eating too many different kinds of food. That may not be healthy. What we need to eat is a good mix of food in the right proportion. A diet is good or healthy if it satisfies all our dietary needs. It must not only have all the nutrients in the correct proportion, but it must also fit into our lifestyle.

So next time you are thinking about dieting, ask yourself the following questions:

❖ Does the diet consist of a variety of food from all the six food groups to supply the nutrients and give a good balance of carbohydrates, proteins and fat?
❖ Does it avoid emphasizing any specific food or group of food?
❖ Is the diet affordable?
❖ Can you use it for long term eating?
❖ Can the whole family use it?
❖ Is there flexibility for individual situations like eating out?

If the answer is 'yes' to all of the above questions, then your diet is worth trying!

ABOUT THE NUTRITIONIST

Dr. Sujata Sunil Udeshi has a Doctorate in Food Science and Nutrition and is associated with Khana Khazana and indiancookery.com as a Nutritionist.

She has set up Diet Department in Inlak Hospital, Pune and Lilawati Hospital, Mumbai.

She specializes in making Nurtition Software, gives advice on health and nutrition to corporates and schools and trains dietitians.

LOW CALORIE ALTERNATIVES TO HIGH CALORIE FOODS

HIGH CALORIE FOOD		LOW CALORIE FOOD	
FOOD ITEM	**CALORIES**	**FOOD ITEM**	**CALORIES**
Whole milk	170 cals/glass	Skimmed milk	80 cals/glass
Aerated drinks	60-80 cals/200ml	Fresh lime juice	0 cals
Lassi (sweet)	250 cals/glass	Plain buttermilk	40 cals/glass
Lassi (salty)	180 cals/glass	"	"
Sherbat	80 cals/glass	"	"
Thick cream soup	200 cals/bowl	Clear soup	40 cals/bowl
Parantha	200 cals	Phulka without ghee	60 cals
Pulao / Fried rice	170 cals/cup	Boiled rice	80 cals/cup
Biryani	250-300/servings	"	"
Fried vegetables	150 cals/cup	Steamed vegetables	70 cals/cup
Coleslaw salad	150-200/serving	Sprouts or vegetable salads	45-80/serving
Regular pudding or dessert	150 cals/serving	Fresh fruit with jelly	40-50 cals/serving
Oil-based dressing	90 cals/tblspn	Lemon dressing	0 cals
Malai paneer	620 cals/100 gms	Low fat paneer	265 cals/100 gms
Double cream (45% fat)	405 cals/100 gms	Skimmed milk	30 cals/100 gms
Normal cream (25% fat)	225 cals/100 gms	"	"
Vegetable sandwich with butter	300 cals/per sandwich	Vegetable samdwich without butter	200 cals/per sandwich
Vagar dhokla	350 cals/serve	Steamed dhokla	200 cals/serve
French fries	350 cals/serve	Boiled/roasted potato	150 cals/serve
Fried cashewnuts	800 cals/serve	Roasted channa	370 cals/100 gms
Fried peanuts	750 cals/serve	"	"
Roasted cashewnuts	600 cals/serve	"	"
Roasted peanuts	570 cals/serve	"	"